YOUR WORD

Also by George Martin:

Reading Scripture as the Word of God (Servant)
Parish Renewal (Servant)
To Pray as Jesus (Servant)
Healing: Reflections on the Gospel (Servant)

Your Word

Scripture Meditations by George Martin

SERVANT BOOKS
Ann Arbor, Michigan

Cover Photo by John B. Leidy

Book Design by John B. Leidy

Scripture quotations are taken from the Revised
Standard Version of the Bible copyright 1946,
1952© 1971, 1973 by the Division of Education
and Ministry of the National Council of Churches in
the U.S.A. and from The Jerusalem Bible © 1966,
1967 by Darton, Longman & Todd and Doubleday
& Co.

Available from Servant Books, Box 8617, Ann Arbor,
Michigan 48107

ISBN 0-89283-090-5

Printed in the United States of America

Contents

Foreword

In the Gospel of John it is written:

> *Then Jesus declared, "I am the bread
> of life. He who comes to me will never
> go hungry, and he who believes in me
> will never be thirsty."*
>
> John 6:35

Jesus feeds us through the Bread of Life and the
Cup of Salvation we receive in the Eucharist.
He also feeds us through the inspired Word of
God. Each of us who has experienced the Spirit
of the living God have a constant hunger for the
Word. We have come to the place of a "felt need"
because we know, through the witness of the
Spirit within, that the scriptures are a sure
guideline for practical living and a norm for
finding the abundant life here and hereafter. The
Bible itself, read in its various approved transla-
tions, provides profound nourishment. But inspired commentary and practical guidance in our
understanding of the Word of God are also
needed to complement that personal wisdom the
Spirit gives each of us when we prayerfully read
the scriptures. George Martin has provided us
with such inspired commentary and practical
guidance in his column "Your Word." It is a gift

to all of us who "hunger and thirst" that some of his columns have been edited into a book for our daily nourishment.

George Martin writes his column, magazine, and books with a balance and wisdom which not only appreciates contemporary biblical scholarship, but also meets the down-to-earth practical needs of busy, family-oriented men and women in the world. Most of us look for uncomplicated moments of inspiration and refreshment. One is always refreshed and renewed reading "Your Word" because what George Martin writes comes from a heart alive to the Spirit and attuned to the realities of everyday life.

Clergy will find George Martin's inspired commentaries a valuable instrument for preparing homilies. Those readers who lament the lack of inspired preaching and teaching from the Word in their particular situation can satisfy their hunger in this book. That a married layman like George Martin should be used by the Lord to feed us is not only an indication of the new work God is doing to shepherd his people, but is also a motivation to us who are ordained elders in the Church to offer our minds and hearts to receive such a gift.

Fr. John Bertolucci

1

It's *Good* News!

*"The beginning of the good news about
Jesus Christ, the Son of God."*
                    (Mark 1:1)

The word "gospel" means "good news." It is
important to realize that the gospel *is* good
news: that the message of Jesus Christ is a message that is truly good news for us.

We can unconsciously fall into thinking of the
gospel as "mixed news": a message that has its
good points and its bad points, its advantages and
its drawbacks. We can welcome those aspects of
the gospel that bring joy and consolation to us—
yet harbor deep seated resentments about other
aspects that make demands on our lives. We can
rejoice that Jesus came to live in our midst—but
resist any suggestion that we are to live in imitation of him.

For some, the gospel can even become "bad
news": a series of impossible demands, a standard of conduct that we cannot measure up to, a
heavy burden that must be carried. If we allow
our own faults and trials and troubles to preoc-
cupy our attention, then the gospel can loom as a
demand that we cannot match up to. Our focus

3

then becomes limited to our unworthiness—an unworthiness that we imagine must incur God's extreme displeasure.

We must constantly remind ourselves that the "good news about Jesus Christ" is *good news*. And it is good news because it does not focus on our sinfulness but on God's love. The good news is that God loves me—and loves me despite my sinful state. The good news is that through Jesus Christ I have been given redemption. The good news is that through the presence of the Holy Spirit in me, God accepts me as his son.

If our eyes are constantly riveted on our own faults, such truths can be hard to accept. If we cannot see much that is lovable in ourselves, we imagine that God cannot either. His eyesight is better than ours, however. And even if he did agree with our assessment of ourselves, it would not stop his love. The really good news is that God loves us anyway, and is willing to go to unimaginable lengths to rescue us from our sin. "What proves that God loves us is that Christ died for us while we were still sinners" (Rom. 5:8).

The gospel is good news because it reveals to me that I do not have to struggle desperately to save myself. On the one hand, I can't rescue myself from sin and death: I simply do not have the power to do so. On the other hand, there is no need for me to even try to earn salvation by my own merits: it has been given to me as a free gift. It's good news to be told that something has been given to us that we could not have obtained by our own efforts.

And yet the gospel does call us to an effort—an effort to live out the life that has been given us. Paul treats both the gift that has been given us and the response we should make to it: "You are God's chosen race, his saints; he loves you, and you should be clothed in sincere compassion, in kindness and humility, gentleness and patience" (Col. 3:12). John likewise views our efforts to love as a response to the prior love of God for us: "This has taught us love—that he gave up his life for us; and we, too, ought to give up our lives for our brothers" (1 John 3:16).

There *is* an element of "bad news" in the gospel. What Jesus has done for me is bad news for the sin within me, for my resistance to love. There is a part of me that must die on the cross with Jesus, in order that I may truly rise with him to eternal life. But just as the surgeon's knife in removing cancer brings life, so the love of Jesus would root out from within us all that causes death.

If we do not think of the gospel as *good news*, we are missing its most basic truths. If we do not think of ourselves as *first of all* sons and daughters of God, we are ignoring the heritage that has been given us. If we do not understand the message of Jesus as above all the assurance that God loves us, we have not heard him correctly and we need to listen afresh to the gospel as "good news."

2

Be Reconciled

> *"I say this to you: anyone who is angry with his brother will answer for it before the court; if a man calls his brother 'Fool' he will answer for it before the Sanhedrin; and if a man calls him 'Renegade' he will answer for it in hell fire. So then, if you are bringing your offering to the altar and there remember that your brother has something against you, leave your offering there before the altar, go and be reconciled with your brother first, and then come back and present your offering."*
>
> (Matthew 5:22-24)

The Gospels were written to preserve a record of the faith that was being lived in the apostolic church. Not every saying or deed of Jesus was set down in writing (John 21:25). Rather, the church remembered and selected those teachings of Jesus that gave guidance for the ongoing life of the church. Thus, the teachings of Jesus which deal with relationships between brothers must be particularly understood as giving direction for how Christians should relate to Christians within the church.

The words of Jesus place a great stress upon unity within the body of Christ. Jesus prayed for the unity of his followers during the Last Supper: "May they all be one, Father, may they be one in us, as you are in me and I am in you, so that the world may believe it was you who sent me" (John 17:21)—a unity so profound that it would be a sign of the divinity of Christ.

Jesus not only prayed for unity among his disciples; he instructed them how their unity was to be preserved. He told them—and he tells us—that there must be no limit to forgiveness: "not seven, but seventy times seven times" must we forgive a brother who wrongs us (Matthew 18:22). We are to be slow in judging others; paying much more attention to the plank in our own eye than the splinter in a fellow Christian's (Matthew 7:1-5).

Jesus accurately identified the ways we are tempted to break unity with other Christians. It is easy to be angry with those whose sloth seems to impede the spreading of the Gospel—but we will have to answer for our anger. It is easy to see the over enthusiastic excesses of some who come to our prayer meetings, and consider these people to be misguided fools—but we will have to answer for our attitudes and actions toward them.

It is all too easy to let seeds of division grow in our midst. We can be inclined to notice that others do not take the exact same approach that we do, and feel that they are somehow less committed or intelligent than we are. We can mistrust those that we are not in steady contact with, simply because we do not understand why they are doing what they are doing. But Jesus' words to us are plain and strong: "John spoke up, 'Master,' he said, 'we saw a man casting out devils in your name, and because he is not with us we tried to stop him.' But Jesus said to him, 'You must not stop him: anyone who is not against you is for you' " (Luke 9:49-50).

We must interrupt even the important duty of worship if we are aware that our brother has something against us, and act to bring about unity again. Jesus seems to make others the judges of our actions: if a brother has something against us, it is up to us to take the first step to be reconciled with him.

If the words of Jesus are to make a difference in our lives, they must make a difference in how we relate to others. They must particularly guide us in our relationships with each other, warning us of the peril of disunity, commanding us to repair whatever disunity does occur.

3

Moses the Reluctant

Yahweh said to Moses, "I send you to Pharaoh to bring the sons of Israel, my people, out of Egypt." Moses said to God, "Who am I to go to Pharaoh and bring the sons of Israel out of Egypt? ... "

Then Moses said to God, "But if they ask me what your name is, what am I to tell them? ... "

Then Moses answered, "What if they will not believe me or listen to my words? ... "

Moses said to Yahweh, "But my Lord, never in my life have I been a man of eloquence, either before or since you have spoken to your servant. I am a slow speaker, and not able to speak well .... "

"If it please you, my Lord," Moses replied, "send someone else."

(Exodus 3 and 4)

One of the most discouraging aspects of our Christian lives can be our awareness that we are not responding to God's call to us with the faithfulness we should. It is sobering to look back over our lives, and realize that our progress has been uneven and slow. We may remember specific instances in which we did not respond as we should have—and we wonder how our lives would be different today if we had.

We can also be pained by our awareness that we are not responding right now as we should. Perhaps we hear the word of the Lord addressed to us through Scripture or prophecy or exhortation—but do not experience his word sinking into us and finding a home. At times his words seem to literally "go in one ear and out the other," and we cannot even clearly remember afterwards what was said. Or at times we may experience a resistence in ourselves to what we hear—a hardness of heart toward what we are asked to do.

Such an awareness can give rise to deep discouragement. "I have always been this way—halfhearted, uncertain, lukewarm in my response—and I guess I always will be." We see others around us eagerly responding to God's call; we wish we were as able to be as quick and wholehearted in our response.

Scripture was written for our encouragement as well as our instruction. It contains a word of consolation to us, as well as a word of exhortation and command. This word of encouragement is often contained in the very lives of those that God has called in the past.

Moses was the greatest leader of the Old Testament. His work, more than the work of any other man, was responsible for the formation of the descendents of Abraham into the people of God. Yet Moses' response to God's call was not always eager and wholehearted. Five times he argued with God, trying to slip out from the service God asked of him.

If God could carry out the greatest work of his plan before the coming of Christ through such a reluctant servant as Moses, he can carry out his will in us and for us despite our uneven response. Our willing response is important, and God does call us on to perfection. But the most basic reality is God's love for us. God does not ask us to be faultless as a condition of his love; he rather asks us to mature as a result of his love. He asks us to make no more response than we are capable of, while giving us the capability to grow in our response through his love.

God does not want his invitation to us to be an impossible standard that we cannot match up to; he does not want his message to us to be merely a source of discouragement. He does want to say to us, "Take heart! I did great things with Moses, and I can do great things even with you. Don't center your attention on your own shortcomings. Focus on my love, and move on with me."

4

God's Timing

*Once David had settled into his house,
he said to the prophet Nathan, "Here
am I living in a house of cedar, while
the ark of Yahweh's covenant is still
beneath the awning of a tent." Nathan
said to David, "Do all that is in your
mind, for God is with you." But that
very night the word of Yahweh came
to Nathan, "Go and tell my servant
David, 'Yahweh says this: You are
not the man to build me a house to
dwell in.' "*

(1 Chronicles 17:1-4)

Once the kingdom was established under David, building a temple to God clearly seemed
to be the proper thing to do. The Israelites no
longer were a nomadic people, migrating about
the middle east in their tents. They had settled
into the promised land, established their cities,
and built their houses. Their possession of the
promised land was more secure than it had been
in the time of the judges. David's military campaigns had united Israel and given it dominance
over its neighbors.

It was no longer fitting to have the ark of the covenant housed in a tent when God's people were living in fine houses. Toward the end of David's life, then, it made sense to build a permanent temple to God. And it made sense to have David build the temple—since it was under his leadership that the kingdom was firmly established in its possession of the land. Nathan, God's chief prophet to Israel at that time, agreed with David's plan to build a temple to God.

Yet God's word to David through Nathan was different. God told David that the time had not yet come for a temple to be built, and that David was not the person chosen by God to build it. Although David had the best of motives, he was not to be God's instrument for building the temple. Although God desired a temple to be built, God's timing for it had not yet arrived.

There is a lesson in this for us today. A certain course of action could make good human sense, and meet with the approval of others—but not be the course of action that God wishes us to take at this time. We might be acting out of the best of motives—yet not be acting in full conformity with the will of God for us.

We are faced with many decisions in the charismatic renewal. Should a city-wide or regional prayer group be split up into smaller groups? Should we begin a prayer meeting in our parish at this time? Should we attempt to form our prayer group into a covenant community? What path should we follow in ecumenism? Should our prayer group make parish renewal its chief concern? How should we have an impact on society?

Many worthwhile courses of action might be open to us. Many of them might be good ideas—and might even be the course of action God wants us to take. But it would still be premature to set out upon them, unless we are proceeding in the Lord's timing. We need to seek God's guidance, not only about what we should do but also about when we should do it.

To try to begin a parish prayer group before the time is ripe, to attempt to form a community before the resources are available, to attempt great things for the Lord before he calls us to do them—all put us ahead of God's timing for us, and ahead of his plan. The apostles were told to preach the gospel to the ends of the earth—but not until they had first waited in Jerusalem for the power of the Holy Spirit to come upon them.

Premature attempts often fail. And after there has been failure, it is sometimes more difficult to try again and succeed, when the time is finally ripe.

God does not want us to be timid, he does not want us to be merely cautious: he wants us to seek his will for us. He wants us to seek his will, not only about what should be done, but when it should be done. God wanted a temple built—but David's plan to build it was premature. God has plans for us and our prayer group—but in his timing. We need to seek his will and be guided by it.

5

The Call to Intercession

This has taught us love—
that he gave up his life for us;
and we, too, ought to give up our
*   lives for our brothers.*

                                  (1 John 3:16)

Few of us will have the opportunity to give up our lives for others in the same way that Jesus totally gave his life for us. But all of us are called to live as he lived. All of us are called to a love which knows no limits, a love which would accept even death itself, should that be asked of us.

To love our brothers as Jesus loves them is a lofty call. It is also a call that can get obscured by the daily routine of our lives, by the complexities of modern society, by the ambiguities of the situations in which we find ourselves. Even if the Holy Spirit has implanted in us a burning desire to love without reserve, translating that desire into effective action can sometimes be difficult.

The more united we become with others in Christian community, the more we become aware of their needs. The more we accept others into our lives as brothers and sisters in the Lord, the more we become aware of areas of hurt in their lives. As we grow in our love for each other, we become increasingly aware of how much more we are called to love.

Sometimes the needs of others can be simply met. We can make an extra effort to speak encouragement to the lonely and insecure; we can visit the sick and bring them meals; we can share our homes with the homeless. But sometimes the needs of others are beyond our ability to meet, and their hurts beyond our capability to heal. We cannot guarantee a safe delivery to a mother experiencing a difficult pregnancy; we cannot fill the void left in a child's life by the untimely death of his mother or father. We sometimes watch helplessly as a marriage breaks up, or as older children reject the love and faith of their parents.

But as Christians we are equipped with an ability to love which goes beyond our own limitations: we are authorized to turn to the Father with our concerns for others. Our love need not be limited by our own capabilities; our love can be expressed in prayer.

Intercession is not a substitute for expressing our love in effective action. Neither should it be a last resort—something we only have recourse to when all else fails. Rather, intercessory prayer should be a dimension of our concern for others and accompany all our attempts to meet their needs. The more intensely we love others, the more aware we should be of the limitations of our love. As we experience the love of God for us, we should increasingly realize how much more perfectly he loves others than we do.

Through his word we know that God welcomes our prayers and hears them. Through experience we know that prayer does make a difference. Through love we are drawn to pray for each other, as an indispensable dimension of our love.

To persevere in daily prayer for others can be truly a laying down of our lives for them. There will be times when we are very attracted to intercessory prayer, and find it a joy. There may also be times when it loses its appeal, and when we are tempted to neglect it. Our faithfulness in daily intercession for the needs of others requires that we put them first, ahead of our comfort or convenience. With steadfast intercession we must "bear one another's burdens, and so fulfill the law of Christ" (Gal. 6:2).

6

Becoming Like Little Children

People were bringing little children to him, for him to touch them. The disciples turned them away, but when Jesus saw this he was indignant and said to them, "Let the little children come to me; do not stop them; for it is to such as these the kingdom of God belongs. I tell you solemnly, anyone who does not welcome the kingdom of God like a little child will never enter it."

(Mark 10:13-15)

The words of Jesus must have startled the disciples: not only were little children to be welcomed into his presence, but they were to enjoy a privileged place in the kingdom of God. In fact, Jesus bluntly warned his followers, "I tell you solemnly, unless you change and become like little children, you will never enter the kingdom of heaven" (Matt. 18:3).

Since Jesus' words indicate a basic requirement for salvation, it is well worth pondering their meaning. Most often, we focus on the qualities which we presume characterize children, and try to imitate them in our lives. Children are thought to be innocent, without guile, direct in their affections, loving, trusting, spontaneous in their emotions, joyful, carefree. We in turn try to make these characteristics a part of our lives, usually without complete success.

Parents know that these traits do characterize children. But parents also know that there is another side to the story. Children can also be unconsciously self-centered, inconsiderate, prey to petty jealousies, indiscriminate in their affections, and inconsistent in their behavior. Whether because of original sin or their parent's shortcomings, most children are not models of virtue —certainly not to the extent that we could understand Jesus making childlike behavior an entrance requirement for the kingdom of God.

If we situate this teaching of Jesus in the context of his other teachings, however, its meaning becomes clearer. The essential characteristic of children that Jesus would have us focus on is their status as sons and daughters. A child is a child of a parent. Whatever the character traits of children might be, whatever stage of moral development they might have attained, the life of small children is essentially defined in terms of their relationship with their parents. Children may be good children or bad children—but they are still sons and daughters. Nothing changes that basic relationship.

The relationship of sonship underlies the parable of the prodigal son. The prodigal did not act

as a good son should have; and even after he re-
pented, he only wished to return to his father's
house as a servant. But the father nevertheless
insisted that he was indeed his son, and gave him
full welcome home. How the prodigal behaved
did not change the basic reality that he was his
father's son—and it did not change his father's
love for him.

Jesus taught us to pray to God as "our Father."
His redemption of us enabled us to enter into a
relationship of sonship with God. "The proof that
you are sons is that God has sent the Spirit of his
Son into our hearts: the Spirit that cries 'Abba,
Father,' and it is that that makes you a son" (Gal.
4:6-7).

What is fundamental in being Christians is the
relationship of sonship that Jesus has established
between us and his Father. What is of primary
importance is our acknowledging that relationship and entering more fully into it. How we be-
have is also important: no parent wants his children to be ill-behaved. But the most basic reality
is simply the reality of sonship.

Interpreted in this light, Jesus is not urging us
to adopt childlike character traits in our life—
much less to act childish. He is urging us to acknowledge the sonship to his Father that he is
giving us. He is saying most solemnly that unless
we enter into sonship, we will not be part of the
kingdom of God. The kingdom of God is the family of the Father, made up of those who have
received adoption as sons through the Spirit of
Christ.

7

Loneliness

All this took place to fulfill the words spoken by the Lord through the prophet: "The virgin shall conceive and give birth to a son and they will call him Emmanuel, a name which means 'God-is-with-us.' "

(Matthew 1:22-23)

The pervading affliction of modern man is loneliness. Technological society works against forming permanent relationships; mobility and freedom bring in their wake an inevitable amount of instability. Our parents lived most of their lives in one city or even one neighborhood; our children can look forward to periodic moves and no permanent home. Their best friend in school last year may have moved across the country during the summer.

The result of such impermanence and rootlessness is a feeling of loneliness. Family life becomes the last bastion of belonging, the last retreat where we can rely on being loved. But even family life lacks ultimate permanence: children grow up and move away; parents become old and die.

God's answer to our deepest longings for love is Jesus Christ. Jesus is Emmanuel: "God-with-us." God is not aloof and unknowable; he bridged the distance between himself and man by becoming man in Jesus of Nazareth. In response to our loneliness, Jesus promises, "I am with you always, even to the end of time" (Matt. 28:20).

Paradoxically, in order for Jesus to remain with us, it was necessary for him to return to his Father: "It is for your own good that I am going, because unless I go, the Advocate will not come to you; but if I go, I will send him to you" (John 16:7). Jesus is present to us now through his Holy Spirit. We can truly apply the same name to the Spirit that Isaiah applied to Christ: Emmanuel, "God-with-us."

Despite the pressures of modern society, despite the separations that inevitably come with time, we do not need to succumb to anxiety or loneliness. We have not been left orphans by Christ; we have rather been incorporated into the family of God, made children of the Father through the presence of the Holy Spirit. In him we find stability; to him we belong; with him we have a permanent home.

Yet more must be said if we are to fully experience the presence of God in our daily lives. Jesus promises that "where two or three meet in my name, I shall be there with them" (Matt. 18:20). The obvious sense of Jesus' words is a promise of his presence when we gather together in his name. But there is another dimension of meaning to his words.

Paul taught that "all of you who have been baptized in Christ have put on Christ" (Gal. 3:27). No longer do we live, but Christ lives in us. When we gather together in the name of Jesus, we do not merely gather as human beings coming into contact with one another. We gather as individuals who by the power of the Spirit have become incorporated into Christ and manifest the presence of Christ in the world today. We gather to be the presence of Christ to each other.

Jesus wishes to heal the loneliness of others not only by the presence of his Holy Spirit, but also through our Spirit-filled presence. He wishes to manifest his love for others through our love for them. He wishes to bring a sense of permanence and stability to their lives not only through his steadfast reliability, but also through our concrete acts of love and concern. The bonds of Christian fellowship we form with others are to be a sign of his bond with them—and an aspect of its reality.

God is with us, through the presence of the Holy Spirit. God is also with us, through our loving presence to each other. We are called to imitate Christ even in his being Emmanuel. God is with us, through us.

8

Take Courage

*Then he got into the boat, followed by
his disciples. Without warning a storm
broke over the lake, so violent that the
waves were breaking right over the
boat. But he was asleep. So they went
to him and woke him saying, "Save
us, Lord, we are going down!" And he
said to them, "Why are you so frightened, you men of little faith?" And
with that he stood up and rebuked the
winds and the sea; and all was calm
again.*

(Matthew 8:23-26)

Jesus often had to exhort his followers to greater
faith, to greater courage in the midst of trying
circumstances. It is significant, however, that
every time Jesus told the disciples to "be not
afraid" they had good reason to be afraid.

Many of the apostles were fishermen, well ac-
quainted with the hazards of storms at sea, well
aware of the dangers of the sea of Galilee. Their
fear during the storm while Jesus slept was a
well informed fear: they were not "landlubbers"

panicking at the sight of a few waves; they were professional sailors who realized they were sinking. Nevertheless, Jesus chided them for being frightened while he was present in the boat.

Jesus' message to the woman who had suffered from a hemorrhage for 12 years was, "Courage, my daughter, your faith has restored you to health" (Matt. 9:22). It did take courage on her part to approach Jesus for healing—first of all, the courage and faith to believe she still could be healed even after having undergone "long and painful treatment under various doctors" which had used up all her money without improving her health (Mark 5:26). Secondly, she needed courage and faith to push her way through a crowd to approach Jesus, despite her suffering from a disease which made her ritually impure, and therefore a social outcast among devout Jews. Jesus' exhortation to have courage was not an idle word, but a message that addressed her need.

Likewise, when Jesus told the apostles, "Do not let your hearts be troubled; trust in God still, and trust in me" (John 14:1), he was speaking to a specific situation in which the apostles had good reason to have troubled hearts: they were eating a last supper with Jesus, on the eve of his death, and had learned that one of his disciples would betray him and another deny him. Yet Jesus told them to continue trusting him despite the apparent disasters that would occur.

In our own lives, we sometimes find ourselves worried or discouraged, anxious or afraid. There are often good reasons why we are worried or afraid; there are sometimes valid grounds for discouragement. To be sure, sometimes our moods seem to be caused by nothing more serious than the weather, and sometimes we become depressed for no apparent reason. Yet at other times we are faced with situations that should be of real concern to us.

When a lingering sickness afflicts our husband or wife, we have good reason to feel concern, and to be humanly fearful of the outcome. When an older child seems to reject his whole training and to turn his back on all his parents taught him, they have ample cause to feel discouraged. When a father loses his job and is unsure how he will support his family, his feelings of anxiety are natural. And if we had been in the boat with the apostles during the storm, we would have been worried too.

Yet in all these situations, the message of Jesus is, "Be not afraid." He does not say that, humanly speaking, everything is going right: he did not deny that there was a storm at sea. He does say that we are not to be fearful even in the face of death itself.

Obviously, our peace cannot then be based on everything going right for us. As in the gospel incidents, our peace must be based on the presence of Jesus in our lives, in his love for us, and his power. Our freedom from fear must be rooted in our faith in Jesus Christ, not in our own ability to handle any problem that might arise.

If we are still victims of fear and anxiety, if we let the circumstances of our lives depress us, it is a sign that our eyes are not firmly enough fixed on Jesus. If we lack an abiding peace, we are not yet fully grounding our lives on God's love for us—a reality that neither human failings nor sickness nor death can overcome.

9

Our Yokes Are Heavy

*"Come to me, all you who labor and
are overburdened, and I will give you
rest. Shoulder my yoke and learn from
me, for I am gentle and humble in
heart, and you will find rest for your
souls. Yes, my yoke is easy and my
burden light."*

(Matthew 11:28-30)

Jesus promised his followers freedom from their
burdens—specifically, the burden of the Mosaic Law with the many additional observances
required by the Pharisees. Rabbis at the time of
Jesus spoke of the "yoke of the Law;" Jesus re-
placed that yoke with a yoke of his own.

Many Christians today are yet overburdened.
It is not the details of Mosaic Law or Pharasaic
regulations which weigh them down; it is rather
the complex demands made by society, job, social group, and family life. Simply to keep up
with the pace of modern life is often a strain; to
try to get ahead and succeed in some endeavor is
even more demanding.

Even our Christianity itself can become a burden to us. Our life can become an unbroken

sequence of meetings, events, and projects—all done in the name of Jesus, but all contributing to a sense of spiritual fatigue. If the pace of modern society is too rapid for our mental tranquility, the busyness with which we go about being Christian can endanger our spiritual well-being.

Our temptation is, at root, the same as that of the Pharisees: to substitute human effort for the saving power of God. The Pharisees sought to fulfill the Law perfectly by multiplying its demands; we can attempt a more Christian life by multiplying meetings and projects. Both attempts are doomed to fail.

Jesus invites those who are overburdened to come to him so that he can *give* them rest. What makes the gospel "good news" is that abundant life is *given* to us as a *gift*. Our "success" in the eyes of God is not something we qualify for by flawlessly keeping a complex set of rules; it is not something we earn by perpetual busyness about many projects. It is first of all a gift, freely given to us by God.

This is not to say that the Christian life is one of unbroken repose. There is a task set before us. Our task is to allow Christ to unite us to himself, and to remake us in his image. This is the "burden" of Christianity.

When we read the words, "my yoke is easy and my burden light," we probably understand Jesus to be speaking of the burden and yoke that he would place on our shoulders. We may even have a mental image of our being yoked to a cart and pulling it, with Christ riding in the driver's seat.

It would be more consistent with the rest of the gospel message, however, to understand these words of Christ in a slightly different way.

When Jesus says, "my yoke is easy and my burden is light," his claim might well be that the yoke he was wearing and the burden he was carrying was light. He would be speaking, in the first instance, of himself carrying the burden of his Father's mission.

In this light, Jesus' invitation to us is an invitation to share his work: to assume the same burden he assumed, to be yoked at his side. Jesus promises that we will find his burden lighter than the false burdens we heap upon ourselves; he tells us that his yoke is a yoke of freedom, easier to bear than the yoke of servitude to sin.

Jesus' invitation is above all the personal invitation, "Come to me." We receive life and freedom as a gift from him; our task as Christians is to undertake the work he was about. But we are first of all invited to become united with him in a personal relationship of faith and love, as the basis of both our rest and our yoke.

10

Doing the Impossible

Then Jesus said to his disciples, "I tell you solemnly, it will be hard for a rich man to enter the kingdom of heaven. Yes, I tell you again, it is easier for a camel to pass through the eye of a needle than for a rich man to enter the kingdom of heaven." When the disciples heard this they were astonished. "Who can be saved, then?" they said. Jesus gazed at them. "For men," he told them, "this is impossible; for God everything is possible."

(Matthew 19:23-26)

Jesus' blunt words about riches were not the only difficult demands he made of his followers. The disciples were often astonished by the requirements of the kingdom; many stopped following Jesus because they could not accept his words.

Jesus taught about the permanence of marriage, and the disciples objected, "If that is how things are between husband and wife, it is not advisable to marry" (Matthew 19:10). If a partner must truly pledge faithfulness in marriage through worse as well as better, then marriage becomes a commitment of one's whole life.

The beatitudes describe the follower of Jesus as poor in spirit, gentle, merciful. Jesus would have us share everything we own with those who are in need. Not only must disciples of Jesus forswear doing violence to others; he asks them to suffer violence at others' hands. Not only is the disciple merciful to his friends; Jesus exhorts, "love your enemies and pray for those who persecute you" (Matthew 5:44).

What Jesus asks of us goes beyond the bounds of the normal, common-sense way we want to run our lives. The rich young man was not leading a sinful life: he had kept the commandments from his youth, he was seeking eternal life. Yet the requirements of discipleship presented by Jesus were too much for him, and "he went away sad" (Matthew 19:22).

In John's gospel, the crowds are faced with their moment of decision in Jesus' teaching about the Eucharist. "I tell you most solemnly, if you do not eat the flesh of the Son of Man and drink his blood, you will not have life in you" (John 6:53). Upon hearing this, "many of his followers said, 'This is intolerable language. How could anyone accept it?' " (v. 60). And after this, "many of his disciples left him" (v. 66). What Jesus asked was too much to believe—even for many who had left their homes to follow after him.

Like the apostles, we may be astonished at what is required of us, and wonder who could possibly measure up to what God expects. Whether

we are asked to adopt a style of life foreign to us, or to obey difficult commands, or to believe in the apparently impossible presence of Jesus in the Eucharist, we seem to be confronted with a demand that is beyond us. We need to hear the commands of Jesus without flinching, and then rely on God to empower us to carry them out. Our call is not to do the impossible, but to trust in the God for whom everything is possible.

11

God's Design

Coming to his home town, Jesus taught the people in their synagogue in such a way that they were astonished and said, "Where did the man get this wisdom and these miraculous powers? This is the carpenter's son, surely? Is not his mother the woman called Mary, and his brothers James and Joseph and Simon and Jude? His sisters, too, are they not all here with us? So where did the man get it all?" And they would not accept him. But Jesus said to them, "A prophet is only despised in his own country and in his own house," and he did not work many miracles there because of their lack of faith.

(Matthew 13:54-58)

It would have been easier for the people of Nazareth to accept Jesus as the Messiah if he had been born into their midst in a fiery chariot, descending from the clouds with an escort of angels. But he was not. He was born into their midst through Mary; he was "the carpenter's son," a descendant of David. In his appearance, he was as any other man. God refused to let his Son appear as anything other than he was: fully human, at the same time that he was divine.

There is a human thirst for the spectacular, for the clearly supernatural, for amazing signs and wonders. And they were present in the life of Jesus—but not as much as his contemporaries would have liked. At the beginning of his ministry, he refused Satan's temptations to turn rock into bread or jump down from the temple pinnacle—although both would have been convincing displays of divine power. And at the end of his ministry, he refrained from calling down 12 legions of warrior angels to defend him. Nor did he heed the cries of the crowd, "If you are God's son, come down from the cross. Let him come down from the cross now, and we will believe in him" (Matt. 27:40, 42).

When Jesus performed the mighty wonder of feeding thousands, crowds flocked after him, and would have made him their king. When he sat down to eat at the same table with sinners, the religious leaders of Israel were shocked. When he performed the lowly service of washing feet, his disciples were embarrassed and confused. When he accepted death as his Father's will for him—death as awaits every human—his followers were scandalized and scattered.

If we had our way, we would remake Jesus into someone more to our liking: someone whose triumph over evil was more obviously complete, someone who does not invite us to suffer in imitation of him. If we had our way, we would redesign Christianity, so that signs and wonders abounded more and patient service less, so that faith came effortlessly and our cross was more comfortable, so that our life was one unending series of joyful triumphs.

But Jesus is the design of the Father for us, and the norm for what it means to be Christian. In his life we find the pattern that we are called to imitate. It is a pattern made up of humble service as well as resurrection. God's pattern for us is a plan that promises us life—but life as he would give it to us.

12

Indiscriminate Love

You have learned how it was said: You must love your neighbor and hate your enemy. But I say this to you: love your enemies and pray for those who persecute you; in this way you will be sons of your Father in heaven, for he causes his sun to rise on bad men as well as good, and his rain to fall on honest and dishonest men alike. For if you love those who love you, what right have you to claim any credit? Even the tax collectors do as much, do they not? And if you save your greetings for your brothers, are you doing anything exceptional? Even the pagans do as much, do they not? You must therefore be perfect just as your heavenly Father is perfect.

(Matthew 5:43-48)

God seems guilty of indiscriminate love. He does not seem to differentiate between those who deserve to have the sun shine upon them and those who do not. If we were charged with

God's responsibility, we would likely pass judgment on the worth of men, and be more discriminating in who received their portion of rain and who did not.

Had we been devout Jews at the time of Jesus, we too would have been scandalized that he associated with those we were taught to reject. "Why does your master eat with tax collectors and sinners?" And Jesus would have given us the same answer he gave the Pharisees: "It is not the healthy who need the doctor, but the sick" (Matt. 9:11-12).

Underlying our attitude toward others is our deeply held belief that we ourselves must, in the final analysis, earn our own salvation. Raised in a society and world that is achievement oriented, we view salvation as one more goal that we need to achieve, and achieve by our own unstinting effort.

If we find ourselves falling short of earning our salvation (as we inevitably must), then we become prey to feelings of guilt and self-condemnation. We have a hard time believing that God loves us despite our failings and unworthiness. We persist in believing that we have to earn the Father's love, instead of accepting it as a free gift.

Consequently, we also have a hard time believing that God loves others as he does. We judge others as we judge ourselves, adding up their good points and bad points, strengths and weaknesses, usually with a keener eye to their failures than their successes. Because we do not rejoice in God's unconditional love for ourselves, we do not believe in his unconditional love for others. And we consequently do not extend our own unconditional love to them.

Yet that is the call of Jesus to us. Not to love others because they deserve our love, but to love them in imitation of the Father. We are called to an indiscriminate love, to a love that does not distinguish between those who deserve our love and those who do not, between enemies that persecute us and brothers that love us in return. Our love is to be as impartial as the sun which rises on bad men as well as good, as the rain which falls on honest and dishonest men alike. We are to love people not as deserving or undeserving, but simply as people. We are to love our enemies not because they are enemies, but simply because they are people and we are to love people. Their being an enemy doesn't change this.

Jesus would in fact call us one step further. He would call us, in imitation of him, to make a special effort to love those who need love most and are therefore the hardest to love. A physician does not enjoy sickness, but he associates with sick people precisely because they are sick. Similarly, those who deserve our love least demand our love most, if we are to sacrifice ourselves in imitation of him who loved us without reserve.

13

The Fruits of Repentance

If you are repentant, produce the appropriate fruits, and do not think of telling yourselves, "We have Abraham for our father," because, I tell you, God can raise children for Abraham from these stones. Yes, even now the axe is laid to the roots of the trees, so that any tree which fails to produce good fruit will be cut down and thrown on the fire.

(Luke 3:8-9)

John the Baptist came clothed in camel skin from the wilderness, challenging the complacency of the sons of Abraham. The word of God came to John in the desert, and the message he proclaimed was no less stark than that desert. The Jews believed that as members of the Chosen People they were the beloved of God. John told them that ancestry was not enough, that mere membership in the Chosen People was not enough. Rather, individual repentance was necessary, a repentance proved by the fruits of one's life.

Jesus acknowledged John as his appointed forerunner, as the one who prepared the way for him. The first proclamation that Jesus issued bears striking resemblance to John's message in both its urgency and thrust: "After John had been arrested, Jesus went into Galilee. There he proclaimed the good news from God. 'The time has come,' he said, 'and the kingdom of God is close at hand. Repent, and believe the good news'" (Mark 1:14-15).

The full message of Jesus has both its contrasts and its similarities with the message of John. John taught that being a son of Abraham was not sufficient for salvation. Jesus came to invite us to enter into sonship of God—and told us that this was in itself salvation. "Eternal life is this: to know you, the only true God, and Jesus Christ whom you have sent" (John 17:3). No human ancestry can qualify us for eternal life, only our adoption as children of God.

Jesus came so that we might become children of God. He came to authorize us to pray to God as "Our Father." The good news that he preached was the news that God loved us, even though we did not deserve his love and could not earn it. Jesus challenged us to believe him, and to accept the sonship he was offering us.

This revelation by Jesus went far beyond the message that John proclaimed. Yet both the message of Jesus and the message of John contain the same command: repent. Change the direction of your life; change the fruit that your life is bearing. John challenged his listeners to become true sons of Abraham. Jesus challenged his followers to become true children of God.

Adoption as sons and daughters of God does not confer on us a status that makes unnecessary all effort on our part. The call of Jesus is a call to receive and accept sonship—and then live out our lives as children of God. Living as a child of God requires change on our part. Our repentance as Christians does not primarily mean conforming to a new set of rules; it primarily means adopting the kind of behavior that is appropriate for a son or daughter of God.

Even in the most sublime teaching of Jesus—the Last Supper discourse presented in the gospel of John—there is an emphasis on keeping the commandments. "If you love me you will keep my commandments. ... Anybody who receives my commandments and keeps them will be the one who loves me" (John 14:15, 21). We can no more use our status as children of God to justify living as we please than the Jews could so use their status as children of Abraham. Both John and Jesus insist that a change in our behavior is necessary, that the true test lies in the fruit that our lives bear.

14

The Temptation to Turn Back

The whole community of the sons of Israel began to complain against Moses and Aaron in the wilderness and said to them, "Why did we not die at Yahweh's hand in the land of Egypt, when we were able to sit down to pans of meat and could eat bread to our heart's content! As it is, you have brought us to this wilderness to starve this whole company to death!"

(Exodus 16:2-3)

Egypt was a land of bitter oppression for the descendants of Abraham. "Groaning in their slavery, [they] cried out for help and from the depths of their slavery their cry came up to God" (Exod. 2:23). God heard their prayers and sent Moses to deliver them. Mighty signs were worked through Moses, and the Israelites were delivered from Egypt. Finally, their freedom came in the parting of the sea and the destruction of the Egyptian army. "Israel witnessed the great act that Yahweh had performed against the Egyptians, and the people venerated Yahweh; they put their faith in Yahweh and in Moses, his servant," and joined in singing a glorious song of victory to Yahweh (Exod. 14:31; 15:1-21).

Their rejoicing and trust lasted all of three days in the wilderness. Then in their thirst they "grumbled at Moses, 'What are we to drink?' " (Exod. 15:24). And water was provided them. Then they grumbled that they were hungry, and manna was provided (Exod. 16). Then they grumbled that they were tired of eating manna ("What are we having for breakfast today?" "Manna." "*Again?*") and longed to return to the fish and cucumbers and melons and onions of Egypt (Num. 11). Always their complaints repeated their longing to return to Egypt: " 'Should we not do better to go back to Egypt?' And they said to one another, 'Let us appoint a leader and go back to Egypt' " (Num. 14:3-4).

The exodus of the Israelites out of Egypt and their time in the desert stand as a pattern of the Christian life. Jesus enjoyed the glory of transfiguration on Mount Tabor—but also knew the agony of crucifixion on the hill of Golgotha. Paul knew the power of Christ in him, even to raising the dead back to life (Acts 21:10-12), but also suffered beatings, shipwreck, hunger, rejection, and imprisonment (2 Cor. 11).

We also may have been granted a glorious experience of God, and a taste of his great love for us. And we may then, after a period of time, have found ourselves in the desert, beset by difficulties that we thought had been resolved long ago.

Egypt was oppression for the Israelites, and their deliverance from it was the most triumphant moment of their existence. Yet in the desert they were only conscious of their thirst and suffering, and longed to return to their slavery. We may have been delivered from a life that was heading for death, and delivered in a way that charged us with enthusiasm for the kingdom of God. Yet in the midst of our present trials and hunger, our past life may look appealing once again. Like the Israelites, we may be tempted to turn back.

That we are so tempted should not surprise us. The experience of the Israelites has been set down in Scripture so that we may learn from it. If, after their triumphal deliverance from oppression, they were tempted to turn back when trials came, we should not be surprised to be similarly tempted ourselves.

But Scripture teaches us that the temptation to turn back must be resisted, no matter how dry the sand of the desert and appealing the delights of Egypt. Scripture also teaches that beyond the desert there is a land promised to us; beyond Good Friday there is Easter morning. Jesus attained to the resurrection because he did not turn back; he promises his resurrection to us, if we persevere in our journey with him.

15

Midday

> *God would not be so unjust as to
> forget all you have done, the love you
> have for his name or the services you
> have done, and are still doing, for the
> saints. Our one desire is that every one
> of you should go on showing the same
> earnestness to the end, to the perfect
> fulfillment of our hopes, never grow-
> ing careless, but imitating those who
> have the faith and the perseverance to
> inherit the promises.*
>
> (Hebrews 6:10-12)

There comes a midday time to the lives of
many dedicated Christians—a time when the
initial enthusiasm of conversion or reconversion
is only a memory, a time when growth in the
Christian life seems to be stalled, a time when
everything seems to be sliding backward into
dry mediocrity. The fire of first love has been
quenched by time and trivia; the goal seems
more distant than ever.

The writers of the New Testament knew about
the temptations that come at the midday of the

Christian life, and wrote words of truth and encouragement to help us remain faithful despite difficulties. The letter to the Hebrews takes a very down-to-earth approach. It reminds us that we can look back upon times in which our commitment to God was uncomplicated and our service to his people was unstinting. Indeed, it reminds us that we are still giving ourselves in service—even if we no longer find the fulfillment for ourselves that we once did in service. And it reminds us that God could hardly be so unjust as to forget all that we have done, to overlook the fact that we once did dedicate our lives completely to him, to ignore all that we have done in his service. We need to believe the truth of Jesus' words, "If anyone gives so much as a cup of cold water to one of these little ones because he is a disciple, then, I tell you solemnly, he will most certainly not lose his reward" (Matt. 10:42), and we need to acknowledge that they apply to our own lives and service.

At the same time, the letter to the Hebrews does exhort us to perseverance and earnestness, to renewed faith and hope. Now is not the time to grow careless; now is the time to imitate those who have remained steadfast to the end. These are not simply empty words, a rhetorical exhortation to be of good cheer. The New Testament acknowledges that there will be trials and temptations, that perseverance will not always be easy, that our faith and hope will be tested. But the New Testament also clearly teaches that we can surmount these trials and temptations in

Christ Jesus: "The trials that you have had to bear are no more than people normally have. You can trust God not to let you be tried beyond your strength, and with any trial he will give you a way out of it and the strength to bear it" (1 Cor. 10:13).

In other words, do not be surprised that you are being tempted as you are. Don't give up at the midpoint of your Christian life, simply because things are no longer as easy as they once were. And do not spend a lot of time bemoaning your newly discovered weakness. Focus rather on the strength of Jesus Christ, given to you so that you can surmount whatever trial or temptation afflicts you.

What distinguishes the New Testament teaching on perseverance and steadfastness is that the focus is not upon ourselves, or upon our own strength. The New Testament insists that our effort is necessary—but it places its emphasis upon God's role rather than upon our own. "It is God, for his own loving purpose, who puts both the will and the action into you" (Phil. 2:13). Therefore, our confidence is not in ourselves (we know how weak we are), but in God, that he will see us through to the end. "God has called you and he will not fail you" (1 Thess. 5:24).

At midday, we can both look back upon the time that has gone before, and look forward to what lies ahead. Because of God's love for us, we can look ahead with confidence and hope: "I am quite certain that the One who began this good work in you will see that it is finished when the Day of Christ Jesus comes" (Phil. 1:6).

16

Christians in Court

> *How dare one of your members take up a complaint against another in the lawcourts of the unjust instead of before the saints? It is bad enough for you to have lawsuits at all against one another: oughtn't you to let yourselves be wronged, and let yourselves be cheated? But you are doing the wronging and the cheating, and to your own brothers.*
>
> (1 Corinthians 6:1, 7-8)

Paul takes the church at Corinth to task for permitting one of its members to bring a civil lawsuit against another member. The matter should have been resolved within the confines of the Christian community. For a Christian, the norm should be not to have lawsuits at all, preferring to be wronged rather than to take legal action against a fellow Christian.

It is easy to nod agreement to Paul's advice, and overlook how different our values are today. How many of us, if we were defrauded of money, would hesitate to sue another person simply because that person was a Christian? If someone refused to pay us a large amount of money that they owed us, would we turn the matter over to our pastor—again, simply because our debtor was a fellow Christian?

Perhaps courts of law were different in Paul's time. The Christian community was certainly different: smaller, more tightly knit, apparently more committed. But do these differences make Paul's teaching completely without point today? Is there something we can still learn from Paul's approach?

Paul's words make sense only if those who follow Christ are joined to one another in some real way. Paul's exhortation makes sense only if we recognize that a bond exists between Christians, a bond at least as strong as the bonds which hold a family together.

If Paul had been writing not to a Christian community but to a family, we would have no problem accepting his solution as a reasonable one. We would agree that there would be something scandalous about a son taking a father to court to redress a wrong, or a brother suing a sister—even if they had a valid case. There is something horribly wrong about members of the same family settling their differences by lawsuits; it indicates a complete breakdown in the bonds which unite a family.

For Paul, those who have found eternal life in Jesus Christ have been joined together by bonds which are even stronger than blood kinship. Paul does not compare the church to a family; he prefers the even stronger analogy of the unity of the human body. Our relationship with Christ makes us members of one body, joined to one another as hand is joined to arm, as sinew to bone. Hence the scandal caused by going to court against a fellow Christian.

Jesus likewise taught that the bonds between his followers were to be even stronger than the bonds of a family. A man is justified in leaving behind father and mother, wife and children, to follow after Jesus (Luke 14:26). For that reason, Jesus' mother and brothers "are those who hear the word of God and put it into practice" (Luke 8:21).

The other side of the coin of willingly "letting ourselves be wronged" is to forgive "seventy times seven times." Most of us will never have occasion to take anyone to court. But we will have many occasions to practice the kind of forgiveness that is necessary in relationships between Christians. Our attitude toward our brothers and sisters in Christ must be one of preferring their good to our own, because we belong to the same family, the same body, the same Lord.

17

Two Prayers

*He spoke the following parable to
some people who prided themselves on
being virtuous and despised everyone
else, "Two men went up to the temple
to pray, one a Pharisee, the other a tax
collector. The Pharisee stood there and
said this prayer to himself, 'I thank
you, God that I am not grasping, unjust, adulterous like the rest of mankind, and particularly that I am not
like this tax collector here. I fast twice
a week; I pay tithes on all I get.' The
tax collector stood some distance
away, not daring even to raise his eyes
to heaven; but he beat his breast and
said, 'God, be merciful to me, a sin-
ner.' This man, I tell you, went home
again at rights with God; the other
did not."*

(Luke 18:9-14)

To understand the full impact of this parable,
we must take the prayers of the Pharisee and
the tax collector at face value: we must assume

they meant what they prayed, and were not simply putting on an act.

The prayer of the Pharisee conveys both the true devotion and tragic flaw of Phariseeism. He did fast twice a week; he was scrupulous in paying tithes on all his income. He was not engaged in a "sinful" occupation, like collecting taxes for Rome, a pagan power. He probably was not a grasping or unjust man; he did not commit adultery. He did give thanks to God for his righteousness: he was in the temple to pray. A good deal of the rest of the world was unjust and adulterous; a good many other Jews were slipshod in their observance of the law. The prayer of the Pharisee contained much truth.

Yet it was not a prayer that met with God's favor. Despite the truth of all the Pharisee prayed, his basic attitude was tragically wrong. His virtue had become a source of pride; he despised anyone who could not live up to the code of conduct that he followed.

The prayer of the tax collector likewise rings true. He was engaged in a "sinful" occupation; he could not come up with an impressive list of religious accomplishments. He was aware that he fell short of fulfilling the law at many points. He consequently felt very sinful, and at a distance from God. He did not pray a prayer of thanks to God; he could only dare a humble prayer of reliance on God's mercy. But his prayer found favor in God's sight.

We too can have characteristics of both the Pharisee and the tax collector. We are aware of the graces we have received from God; we are aware that we are leading lives which are virtuous when compared with the ways of the world. But we can sometimes fall into viewing others through a Pharisee's eyes, subtly looking down upon them because they have not experienced what we have experienced, or do not follow the way of life we do. The parable must be a stiff reminder that no matter how favored and virtuous we are, and no matter how misguided and sinful the world is, we earn God's judgment by falling into an attitude which despises others.

We can also find ourselves praying as the tax collector prayed—aware of how far we fall short of God's plan for us, feeling at a distance from God, unable to pray a prayer of thanksgiving or praise with any conviction. The prayer of the tax collector was hardly very "pentecostal"; he probably would not have felt very much at home in a charismatic prayer meeting. Yet his prayer was found acceptable by God. God viewed him more favorably than the tax collector viewed himself. God honored his cry for mercy. God will likewise hear our prayers for mercy—no matter how unholy we feel, no matter how aware we are of our sins, no matter how distant we feel ourselves to be from God.

18

Chosen Anyway

The disciples had forgotten to take any food and they had only one loaf with them in the boat. Then he gave them this warning, "Keep your eyes open; be on your guard against the yeast of the Pharisees and the yeast of Herod." And they said to one another, "It is because we have no bread." And Jesus knew it, and he said to them. "Why are you talking about having no bread? . . . Have you eyes that do not see, ears that do not hear? Or do you not remember? When I broke the five loaves among the five thousand, how many baskets full of scraps did you collect?" They answered, "Twelve." . . . Then he said to them, "Are you still without perception?"

(Mark 8:14-19, 21, *JB*)

The gospel portrait of the first followers of Jesus is, on the balance, an unflattering picture. The gospels do record confessions of faith in Christ: Peter's, "You are the Christ, the Son of the living God" (Matt. 16:16), and Mary's, "I believe that you are the Christ, the Son of God, the one who was to come into this world" (John 11:27). But there are also numerous instances where the faith of Jesus' followers was weak, where they were slow to understand his message, where they were ruled by fear.

Many times the disciples simply failed to understand the teachings of Jesus. They had to approach him privately to have him explain the meaning of parables (Matt. 13:36). They were sometimes shocked by his message: "When the disciples heard this they were astonished, 'Who can be saved then?' they said" (Matt. 19:25). And they were very slow to understand his coming death and resurrection. Luke recounts three different times that Jesus foretold his coming passion. Yet even after the third explanation the apostles "could make nothing of this; what he said was quite obscure to them, they had no idea what it meant" (Luke 18:34).

The dullness of the apostles continued right to the end. At the last supper, even after Jesus had shared his body and blood with them, they fell into a dispute over which of them was the most important (Luke 22:24). Jesus tried to warn Peter that he would be severely tested, but Peter brushed his words aside with bluster and bravado. Jesus told the apostles to be ready for a time of crisis, and they reassured him that they were indeed prepared for it, that they had two swords—completely misunderstanding the nature of the coming trial (Luke 22:38).

It is as if Jesus had not picked the most qualified and promising people to be his disciples, but had instead simply asked people at random to follow him. Normally the leader of a new cause will want to surround himself with talent; Jesus, on the other hand, seemed to select a group of people that were unremarkable. The Pharisees dismissed the followers of Jesus as being rabble, "tax collectors and sinners" (Luke 7:34). Perhaps their judgment was not that far off the mark.

And that is good news for us. No matter how slow we seem to be in growing to maturity of faith, no matter how frail we seem to ourselves, no matter how discouraged we become, we are in good company. The first followers that Jesus chose were no more adept at following him than we are. They found eternal life, not because they earned it, but because Jesus chose them.

Jesus has also chosen us, and asked us to follow him, despite our weaknesses. No doubt he could have chosen more competent people. But he chose us.

19

The Final Exam

One of the criminals hanging there abused him. "Are you not the Christ?" he said. "Save yourself and us as well." But the other spoke up and rebuked him. "Have you no fear of God at all?" he said. "You got the same sentence as he did, but in our case we deserved it: we are paying for what we did. But this man has done nothing wrong. Jesus," he said, "remember me when you come into your kingdom." "Indeed, I promise you," he replied, "today you will be with me in paradise."

(Luke 23:39-43, *JB*)

There were once two teachers teaching in a school. The first teacher did not enjoy teaching, and did not really care for students. His lectures were dull, yet he disciplined his class if they did not pay attention. Before school let out each year, he would administer a very long and difficult final exam. It was designed to uncover everything the students hadn't learned, and he graded it very strictly. Students lived in dread all year of the exam they would face at the end.

The second teacher genuinely loved students, and worked very hard to help them learn. His greatest joy came when a student did grasp a new idea, or succeeded in learning a new skill. He spent extra time with those who had the hardest time learning. He liked to be around students, and invited them over to his house for dinner. He also gave a final exam each year, but he designed it to find out what his students had learned, not what they hadn't learned. There were no trick questions, and his students knew that he was eager for them to pass it.

If we were to imagine God to be a teacher, we might have a tendency to imagine him to be the first kind of teacher. We might imagine God tolerating man, but not really finding enjoyment in him. Life in the cosmic classroom of this teacher would be bound by many rules and we could expect sure punishment if we disobeyed any of them. We would be very unsure that we would pass the final judgment of this teacher, and we would live our lives in quiet dread of the day we would have to face it.

Jesus came to teach us about God, and he did it by being a faithful mirror of his Father. The God that he revealed by his life was not like the first teacher but rather the second.

Jesus found delight in being with us: "Zacchaeus, come down. Hurry, because I must stay at your house today" (Luke 19:5). He did not hold himself aloof from sinners, but sought them out with a special concern. "It is not those who are well who need the doctor, but the sick" (Luke 5:31). Jesus did not aim at catching someone in their sin, but at delivering them from sin. " 'Has no one condemned you? . . . Neither do I condemn you . . . Go away, and don't sin any more' " (John 8:10, 11). Just as the second teacher found joy in his students learning, so Jesus found joy in his disciples coming to know God: "It was then that, filled with joy by the Holy Spirit, he said, 'I bless you, Father, Lord of heaven and earth, for hiding these things from the learned and the clever and revealing them to mere children' " (Luke 10:21).

Jesus also taught us that the eternal judgment to be made by his Father will be like the final exam of the second teacher. There will be no trick questions. God will not be aiming at finding enough fault in us to condemn us, but enough faith to reward us.

The thieves who were crucified with Jesus had led lives of crime. One of them, however, admitted that his punishment was deserved, and asked Jesus to remember him in his kingdom. His request was a very simple act of faith, but the response of Jesus was unconditional: "Indeed, I promise you, today you will be with me in paradise." No one else in the gospel accounts receives such firm assurance of salvation from Jesus. And by our standards, no one deserved it less! But Jesus did not focus on the life of crime that this man had led; Jesus only focused on his few simple words of faith. It was as if a teacher knew that a student had only learned one thing all year, and therefore asked only that question on the final exam.

"For God sent his son into the world not to condemn the world, but so that through him the world might be saved" (John 3:17).

20

The Strength of Clay

It is not ourselves that we are preaching, but Christ Jesus as the Lord, and ourselves as your servants for Jesus' sake. It is the same God that said, "Let there be light shining out of darkness," who has shone in our minds to radiate the light of the knowledge of God's glory, the glory on the face of Christ. We are only the earthenware jars that hold this treasure, to make it clear that such an overwhelming power comes from God and not from us.

(2 Corinthians 4:5-7)

Archaeologists digging up the remains of ancient cities in Palestine inevitably discover great quantities of broken clay jars. By tracing the changes through time in the design of jars, scholars can reconstruct the rise and fall of kingdoms, the migration of peoples, the destruction of nations.

Clay was the most commonly used building material in the ancient Near East. Clay could be molded into bricks and left to dry in the sun, and buildings could be made from these bricks. Clay could be formed into pots and dishes and water jugs, and baked in simple furnaces. Those who could not afford houses of wood and stone lived in houses of clay. Those who could not afford jugs of metal carried their water in earthenware jars.

Earthenware jars were fragile. If they were dropped, they shattered. Replacing them was an easy matter: clay was almost as common as the dirt at one's feet. Bronze jugs were much more sturdy and much more valuable—but at a cost that many could not afford.

Paul used this fact of everyday life to illustrate one of the paradoxes of the gospel. We have been given a great treasure: life in Jesus Christ. But we carry this treasure in the common clay pot of ourselves. It is as if a wealthy man kept a supply of the most costly ointment in the world in a rude and cracked clay pot.

We know our unworthiness before God's glory. Clay is not worthy to hold precious ointment; bronze or gold should be used. But we are clay, and the glory of God has been poured into our lives nonetheless. We know our chips and cracks, we know where our lives are out of round. Yet despite this, the treasure of the Holy Spirit has been given to us. Clearly God does not love us because we have earned his love, but because he is love.

We also know our weakness and fragility. If a clay pot is bumped off the table, it shatters and its contents are spilled out onto the dust of the floor. If something should drop on an earthenware jar, it crumbles into pieces. God's life has been poured into us, but we remain earthenware jars nonetheless. The power that is manifest in our lives does not come from ourselves, but from the treasure that we carry. We are not brass jugs, capable of surviving knocks and blows through stoical determination. We are clay jars, dependent on God's protection for our survival.

It is well to acknowledge the source of our strength; it is also well not to overemphasize our weakness. The fact that archeologists may yet today discover whole jars and pots that have survived over 2,000 years is a testimony to the staying power of common clay. Iron rusts, wood burns, but clay endures. So with us. Most of us underestimate our inner resources, our capability for surviving hardship, our ability ever to begin anew to reshape our lives according to God's call. We are fragile—but not fragile like a flower. Our endurance is limited—but it is a real endurance. God's power operates in our weakness—but not in our despair.

> *We are in difficulties on all sides, but never cornered; we see no answer to our problems, but never despair; we have been persecuted, but never deserted; knocked down, but never killed; always, wherever we may be, we carry with us in our body the death of Jesus, so that the life of Jesus, too, may always be seen in our body.*
>
> (2 Corinthians 4:8-10)

21

Comfort in Exile

For I, Yahweh, your God,
I am holding you by the right hand;
I tell you, "Do not be afraid,
I will help you."

Do not be afraid, Jacob, poor worm,
Israel, puny mite.
I will help you—it is Yahweh who
*   speaks—*
the Holy One of Israel is your
*   redeemer.*

(Isaiah 41:13-14)

These words of consolation were apparently addressed to the Israelites during their time of exile in Babylon. If the descendants of Abraham ever needed a message of hope and consolation, it was at this time, when all their political hopes had been shattered and their beloved Jerusalem destroyed.

God had appeared to Abraham at Shechem and promised to give the land of Canaan to his descendants. God spoke to Moses from the burning bush, and promised to give his people "a land rich and broad, a land where milk and honey

flow, the home of the Canaanites" (Exod. 3:8).
God renewed this promise from Mount Sinai,
after establishing the covenant, and repeatedly
reminded his people of it as they were entering
the promised land.

Within the promised land, Jerusalem occupied
a place of prominence. After David conquered it,
he made it his capital and moved the Ark of the
Covenant there. His son Solomon built the great
temple in Jerusalem, which became the center of
worship for the chosen people.

Then hard times came. Division split the chosen people into the Northern Kingdom and the
Southern Kingdom. The divided kingdoms were
not able to preserve the political independence
the people had under David; nor was either
kingdom ever able to recapture the splendor of
Solomon's reign.

The Northern Kingdom fell to the armies of
Assyria in 721 B.C., and massive deportations
took place. Jerusalem and the Southern Kingdom maintained a precarious existence until 587,
when Jerusalem was destroyed by the armies of
Babylon, and its citizens carried off into exile.
The kingdom of David was no more; the temple
of Solomon was reduced to rubble.

Had God abandoned his people? Had he taken
back his promises? Had he forgotten his covenant? How could he allow his people to be so
thoroughly devastated, to be left in such a pitiful
state?

God had not abandoned his people; he was still faithful to his covenant. In very few years, Cyrus the Persian would conquer Babylon and allow the exiles to return home to Jerusalem. The temple would be rebuilt; once more Zion would ring with psalms.

But in the depths of exile, the captives had difficulty foreseeing this rescue. Hope came hard. The captives were only aware of their own weakness and suffering. Their pain made little sense to them. Nothing had gone according to plan.

God's word reassured them: "I am holding you by the right hand; do not be afraid." Do not focus on your own weakness, as poor and puny as you are, but on him who helps you: "the Holy One of Israel is your redeemer." I have a love for you which goes beyond your understanding, a plan for you which surpasses your vision.

While few of us today are so sorely afflicted as the Israelites during their time of exile, we are put to the test in different areas of our lives. Things often do not go according to our plans and expectations. Divisions separate one Christian from another. The works of God that we so eagerly dedicate ourselves to are sometimes dashed to the ground, like the temple of Jerusalem. We have a hard time understanding God's plan from the midst of our disappointment and pain; we are tempted to lose hope. The appearance of our lives seems to gainsay the promises we have received from God.

God's word to us is the same as his word to the Israelites in exile:

> *You are my servant,*
> *I have chosen you, not rejected you.*
> *Do not be afraid, for I am with you;*
> *stop being anxious and watchful, for I am*
> *your God.*

(Isaiah 41:9-10)

22

The Joy and Power
of the Spirit

*The seventy-two came back rejoicing.
"Lord," they said, "even the devils
submit to us when we use your name."
He said to them, "I watched Satan fall
like lightening from heaven. Yes, I
have given you power to tread underfoot serpents and scorpions and the
whole strength of the enemy; nothing
shall ever hurt you. Yet do not rejoice
that the spirits submit to you; rejoice
rather that your names are written in
heaven.*

(Luke 10:17-20)

Two of the earmarks of the presence of the
Holy Spirit are power and joy.

The gospel according to Luke ends with Jesus
telling the apostles that the time has come for
them to receive the Holy Spirit that had been
promised them: "Stay in the city then, until you
are clothed with the power from on high" (Luke
24:49). And the Acts of the Apostles begins with
a similar instruction: "You will receive power

when the Holy Spirit comes on you, and then you will be my witnesses" (Acts 1:8).

Power is not something imaginary. Power is something real, something that makes a difference. A strong man has the power to lift heavy weights; a weak man does not. If the weak man should claim that he has as much power as the strong man, we could very simply put him to the test: either he could lift the weights the strong man could lift, or he could not. If he could not, we would deny his claim that he had power.

The power of the Holy Spirit likewise makes a difference. When the Holy Spirit comes to us, he does not hide in the depths of our soul, silent and undetectable. He manifests himself in our lives, in our attitudes, in the way we act, in what we are able to do. If someone were to claim that he had the power of the Spirit, but that it made no difference in his life, we would have to wonder what his claim meant.

Real power must be the power to do something, to be something. The power of the Spirit is the power to be Christlike, to follow in the footsteps of Jesus, to act with his authority, to love with his love. The power of the Spirit enables us to do what we could never do on our own.

The seventy-two came back from their mission amazed that they had a power that they had not known before. Jesus had given them a foretaste of the power of the Spirit, "power to tread underfoot serpents and scorpions and the whole strength of the enemy." And they found that "even the devils submit to us when we use your name." This was not imaginary power; this was real power, whose effect could be observed.

Consequently, they rejoiced. The working of the Spirit in them brought a joy they had not known before. Paul lists joy as a fruit of the Spirit (Gal. 5:22): it is an indication of the working of the Holy Spirit in our lives. Jesus told the seventy-two that they should not rejoice so much over the external manifestations of the power of the Spirit, but over his fundamental work in their lives. By the presence of the Spirit within us we are adopted as children of God, able to pray to our Father as "Abba." By the action of the Spirit our names are written in heaven, as the chosen of the Father. This is great cause for rejoicing.

We know from experience that the Christian life is not one unbroken string of happy events. Paul urged Timothy to "bear the hardships for the sake of the good news, relying on the power of God" (2 Tim. 1:8). Our joy cannot be based on external circumstances, but must be based on the presence and power of the Spirit within us.

Nor does the power of the Spirit mean that we shall effortlessly vanquish every problem that confronts us. Paul learned through painful experience that the power of God operates in our weakness (2 Cor. 12:9). If we are to imitate Jesus in his resurrection, we must first follow him to Calvary.

Nevertheless, our lives should be marked by a power and joy that we experience as a gift from God—a power and joy that goes beyond our natural strength, a joy that is not dependent on circumstances. The gift of the Spirit must make a manifest difference in our lives, empowering us to be witnesses that the gospel is indeed good news, making us rejoice that we have been chosen to be children of God.

23

Stand Up and Walk

*Some men appeared, carrying on a bed
a paralyzed man. . . . Jesus, aware of
their thoughts, made them this reply,
"What are these thoughts you have in
your hearts? Which of these is easier:
to say, 'Your sins are forgiven you,' or
to say, 'Get up and walk'? But to prove
to you that the Son of Man has authority on earth to forgive sins"—he
said to the paralyzed man—"I order
you: get up, and pick up your stretcher
and go home." And immediately before their very eyes he got up, picked
up what he had been lying on and
went home praising God.*

(Luke 5:18, 22-25, *JB*)

The burdens we carry through life can be an
assortment of spiritual and physical debili-
ties: habits we cannot break, physical sickness,
bondage to our emotions, ingrained patterns of
destructive behavior. Jesus went among us curing the sick, and promised us abundant life in his

Spirit. We therefore can turn to him for the healing and freedom we need.

Jesus did not employ any one means or formula for curing the sick. Some he healed by a touch, some he made whole by casting out a demon, some he commanded: "Be cured," and some he simply told to "Stand up." The man by the Pool of Bethzatha was ordered to "Get up, pick up your sleeping-mat and walk" (John 5:8).

Jesus today would also have us confront many of our debilitating infirmities by a resolve to "get up and walk." The healings that he wishes us to have depend on our resolve to be whole as well as upon his power to heal.

This does not mean that we can simply "claim a healing" and ignore physical symptoms of sickness. But many of the illnesses we suffer from are not primarily physical, even if they sometimes have physical by-products. We can be almost as paralyzed by depression as was the man brought to Jesus on the stretcher. We can be crippled by painful memories from our past; we can be bound by bad relationships with our family or with others; we can find our life hemmed in by destructive habits we have acquired over the years.

For many of these kinds of infirmity, Jesus' word to us is, "Stand up." His healing touch operates through our own resoluteness and action. If our attitude is, "I'm so emotionally crippled by my past that I really can't act as a Christian should," we will remain emotionally crippled. But if our attitude is, "I am going to act as I know I should, despite the pain I have suffered in the past," then we will cooperate with Jesus in the healing that he will work within us.

This is not to say that we can simply force ourselves to be healthy by sheer willpower. It is to say that the healing word that Jesus may wish to address to us is the command, "Get up and walk." He may wish to say to us, "Don't focus on your illness, but on obedience to my will for you. Don't use your emotions as an excuse for not behaving as you should, but act as you know you ought to, despite how you feel."

This is not a harsh word from Jesus, but a healing and freeing word. He does not require the impossible from us; rather, he requires from us the cooperation on our part which will allow full healing to take place.

When the woman caught in adultery was brought before Jesus, he displayed great tenderness and forgiveness toward her. He refused to condemn her. But he did say, "Don't sin any more" (John 8:11). He ordered her to step out of her life of sin and begin obeying God's commandments for her life.

When the paralytic on the stretcher was let down through the roof, Jesus granted him a healing of spirit as well as body: he forgave him his sins, as well as curing his physical illness. But he did command him to get up, and pick up his stretcher and go home, and get on with his life. His message to us may be the same: "Stand up, take authority over your problems, and follow after me in your daily life."

24

Time for Prayer

> *In the morning, long before dawn, he
> got up and left the house, and went off
> to a lonely place and prayed there.
> Simon and his companions set out in
> search of him, and when they found
> him they said, "Everybody is looking
> for you."*
>
> (Mark 1:35-37)

It can scarcely surprise us that Jesus prayed. What is striking, however, is the difficulty Jesus had in finding the time and solitude to pray, and the determination he showed in overcoming this difficulty.

Jesus attracted crowds wherever he went. Sometimes the crowds were so thick that a crippled man on a stretcher could not be brought through, and had to be lowered from the roof into Jesus' presence (Luke 5:17-26). In the background of the gospel narratives there always are crowds of people coming to Jesus with their needs. "He went home again, and once more such a crowd collected that they could not even have a meal" (Mark 3:20).

When Jesus and the apostles wished to be alone, their only alternative was to try to steal away—a tactic that did not always work:

"Then Jesus said to them, 'You must come away to some lonely place all by yourselves and rest for a while'; for there were so many coming and going that the apostles had no time even to eat. So they went off in a boat to a lonely place where they could be by themselves. But people saw them going, and many could guess where; and from every town they all hurried to the place on foot and reached it before them" (Mark 6:31-33).

Such a life-style hardly seems conducive to prayer. Our image of a life oriented to prayer is one of unhurried pace, regular schedule, silence, solitude. In contrast, the life of Jesus was akin to that of a presidential candidate: always in the public eye, never far from the clamor of the crowds, continually travelling from one place to another. "The Son of Man has nowhere to lay his head" (Luke 9:58).

Yet Jesus did spend time in prayer. Sometimes he would send the apostles and the crowd on ahead, while he would go up into the hills to pray (Mark 6:45-46). Sometimes he arose early in the morning; sometimes he stayed up late, praying far into the night. "Large crowds would gather to hear him and to have their sickness cured, but he would always go off to some place where he could be alone and pray" (Luke 5:15-16).

We can learn the way of prayer from Jesus, and draw encouragement from his life of prayer. If we must contend with erratic schedules and the demands of family life, so did Jesus contend with the demands of those who came to him for instruction and healing. If the pace of modern life seems too rapid to allow us the luxury of prayer, the public ministry of Jesus was no less hectic. If we have trouble finding a quiet place alone with God, Jesus experienced the same difficulty. If our job demands a lot of us, Jesus' ministry demanded no less of him.

The example of Jesus teaches us that we need frequent times of communion with his Father. It also teaches us that we may have to overcome obstacles in order to have this time. The ideal would be for us to have a regular time for prayer in our daily schedule. In reality, we may have to make time as best we can each day. The tenacity with which Jesus made time for his prayer must be our model; his determination to pray must be before our eyes as we set out to create a prayer time for ourselves.

The example of Jesus is also reassuring. We may feel guilty because our prayer time is irregular, because our day is fragmented by hundreds of demands by small children, because our solitude is invaded by traffic jams and factory whistles. Jesus knows that ours is not the life of a 12th-century monk. He will understand our failures, if only we set out to make time for prayer with the same determination he had in finding time to be with his Father.

25

Jonah

> *The word of Yahweh was addressed to*
> *Jonah son of Amittai: "Up!" he said,*
> *"Go to Nineveh, the great city, and*
> *inform them that their wickedness has*
> *become known to me." Jonah decided*
> *to run away from Yahweh, and to go to*
> *Tarshish.*
>
> (Jonah 1:1-2, *JB*)

Jonah is sometimes remembered only for having been in the belly of the fish for three
days—which almost makes the fish the central
character of the story. But the book of Jonah contains an important message about God's plan of
salvation.

The book of Jonah is short (only 48 verses) and
its story is simple. God wishes to send Jonah to
Nineveh with his word. Nineveh was the capital
of the Assyrian empire, a hated enemy that had
conquered and deported the Northern Kingdom
of Israel in 721 B.C. At the thought of taking
God's message to the enemies of Israel, Jonah
flees. But a storm at sea and a great fish bring

Jonah back, and God a second time orders Jonah to go to Nineveh.

Jonah does obey this time, and delivers God's message of judgment: "Only forty days more and Nineveh is going to be destroyed" (Jonah 3:4). But to Jonah's amazement the inhabitants of Nineveh repent in sackcloth and ashes, and God forgives them. This makes Jonah indignant: he did not want God to be "a God of tenderness and compassion, slow to anger, rich in graciousness, relenting from evil" (Jonah 4:2); he had been looking forward to Nineveh's destruction. But God defended his mercy: "Am I not to feel sorry for Nineveh?" (Jonah 4:11).

The book of Jonah was written to correct a narrow nationalism that tempted the chosen people after the exile. Firm resolve had been needed to rebuild the walls of Jerusalem, and great emphasis was placed on restoring the worship of Yahweh in all its purity. The laws of the covenant were strictly imposed again, and foreign-born wives were sent away. While these measures were necessary to restore Judaism after the exile, they also had an unfortunate side effect: the Israelites were in danger of turning in upon themselves and becoming blind to the larger dimensions of God's love and mercy. Israel was in danger of viewing itself as the only people called by God.

The book of Jonah was written as a corrective to this narrowness of vision. God's word comes to the Israelite Jonah, but he does everything he can to evade God's mission for him. God's word

comes to Nineveh, the pagan city, and they immediately repent in sackcloth! Jonah is upset that
God shows them mercy: weren't they the enemy?
God defends his compassion and mercy, and the
universality of his love.

We today can need to be reminded of the
breadth of God's love, and the far-reaching in-
tent of his plan. To the very extent that God
has blessed us personally, or selected our group
for his mission, there can arise a temptation to
narrowness of vision. Particularly if we have to
struggle to accomplish what God has called us to,
and if we have to defend it against attacks or misunderstanding, we can be tempted to view what
God is doing in our midst as his most significant
presence in the world today. As a result, we may
be blind to the other ways he is acting to accomplish his purpose. In our effort to be faithful to
what he has called us to do, we can be less sensi-
tive to the different ways that he has chosen to
work in others.

The book of Jonah can be a reminder that
God's plan is always greater than our understanding, and God's love always beyond our com-
prehension. It can be a warning against letting
a narrowness of vision infect us. And it can be
an encouragement to us: God is indeed a God
of mercy and compassion, concerned about even
those "who cannot tell their right hand from
their left, to say nothing of all the animals"
(Jonah 4:11).

26

Inconsistencies

> *To my friends I say: Do not be afraid
> of those who kill the body and after
> that can do no more. I will tell you
> whom to fear: fear him who, after he
> has killed, has the power to cast into
> hell. Yes, I tell you, fear him. Can you
> not buy five sparrows for two pen-
> nies? And yet not one is forgotten in
> God's sight. Why, every hair on your
> head has been counted. There is no
> need to be afraid: you are worth more
> than hundreds of sparrows.*
>
> (Luke 12:4-7, JB)

Sometimes the words of Scripture can strike us
as inconsistent, though we believe in faith
that they are not. Jesus frees a man from demons
and instructs him to go home and "report all that
God has done for you" (Luke 8:39). But short-
ly thereafter, when Jesus raises the daughter of
Jairus back to life, he gives him orders "not to tell
anyone what had happened" (Luke 8:56).

Presumably Jesus had his reasons for asking
one person to bear witness and another to hush
up a great miracle (and a difficult miracle to hide:

how do you conceal the fact that your daughter has been raised from the dead, after there has already been a crowd mourning her death?). But at first reading, Jesus appears to take an inconsistent approach to the question of testifying to cures.

Jesus' attitude toward the law of Moses is also puzzling. The constant criticism of the Pharisees was that Jesus and his followers disregarded the law, particularly the observance of the sabbath. Jesus *did* take a radical stance to the question of sabbath observance: "The sabbath was made for man, not man for the sabbath" (Mark 2:27). Yet Jesus also taught, "It is easier for heaven and earth to disappear than for one little stroke to drop out of the Law" (Luke 16:17). The early church had to wrestle with this issue when it had to decide whether gentile converts to Christianity were bound by all the requirements of the law of Moses. The issue was a difficult one to resolve; witness the discussions of Peter and Paul (see Acts 15).

Jesus' teaching on our basic attitude toward God also poses a challenge. On the one hand we are told to fear God, who "has the power to cast into hell." On the other hand, we are told, "there is no need to be afraid"; God has concern even for sparrows, and we are much more valuable in his sight. Which injunction are we to take as normative: to fear God, or not to be afraid?

It is dangerous to take any one text from Scripture as *the* word of Scripture on a subject. Not only must we read individual passages in context, we must also read passages that balance, and sometimes seem to contradict each other, in order to get the full teaching of Scripture.

There are two discernible strands of teaching in Scripture regarding fear of God: one that insists God will bring sure judgment on all who disobey him, and another that portrays God as a loving Father, eager to forgive. If we read only the condemnations in the prophetic books, we will get an insight into only one aspect of God. If we read only the parable of the prodigal son, we will get a different partial glimpse. We must read both types of passages in order to gain an understanding of God as both just judge and forgiving Father.

There is, therefore, a sense in which fear of God is important: we must recognize that he is God and we are but his creatures, that it is his right to command and our duty to obey. But there is also a sense in which we should not approach God in fear: he is our loving Father in heaven, and is no more eager to consign us to eternal fire than we would be to condemn our own children to such a fate.

The words of Jesus are not inconsistent, but they do bring out complementary aspects of a mystery. The mind of man cannot grasp the mystery of God's plan all at once; we must consider different facets of it. We are able to see only in part, as "a dim reflection in a mirror" (1 Cor. 13:12). We must not seize any one glimmer of truth as the whole truth. We must try to be faithful to the whole of revelation, even if that demands our wrestling with complexities and seeming inconsistencies.

27

Division

If you go snapping at each other and tearing each other to pieces, you had better watch or you will destroy the whole community.

(Galatians 5:15, *JB*)

Throughout the ages thoughtful men have somberly contemplated the mystery of evil. Why is there sickness and suffering, disease and death? Why does mankind destroy itself in war? Why does one human make another human the object of prejudice, scorn, hatred? Why is there evil in our own hearts?

Scripture gives answers to these questions. Genesis teaches that the evil in our midst is the work of man, not of God. Paul tells us that our battle is not merely against flesh and blood, but against principalities and powers. Jesus made himself subject to suffering and death, so that we might rise with him to eternal life. The answers of Scripture do not completely remove the pain or mystery of suffering: we still must live by faith; we still see as in a mirror, darkly.

The mystery of evil is nowhere more incomprehensible than when it touches upon the very plan of God. The alienation of one human being from another is never easy to accept, but it becomes incomprehensible when the parties in strife are Christian. Mistrust and hostility become even more painful when they exist between those who call upon God as their Father.

Yet the history of God's people is a history of division and strife. The kingdom of David and Solomon was the high point of Hebrew military might and political splendor, but it was shot through with palace intrigues and the plotting of brother against brother. At the death of Solomon, the division of the nation into the southern kingdom of Judea and the northern kingdom of Israel marked the end of the Hebrews as a united people, and the beginning of their long decline into foreign servitude.

At the time of Jesus, divisions within Judaism were manifest. Samaritans were rejected as racially impure heretics; Galileans were scorned as country bumpkins. The religious establishment of Judaism was split along party lines. The Sadducees and Pharisees addressed questions to Jesus, not to learn the truth, but to score debating points against each other.

How would the history of God's people be different if the descendents of Abraham had remained one people of pure allegiance to God? How would the New Testament read if Jesus had not been dismissed as a Galilean by the religious leaders of Jerusalem, and if the factions had been of one mind to seek the truth together?

No wonder Paul's special wrath was reserved for those who sowed division in the early church: "I wish those who unsettle you would mutilate themselves!" (Gal. 5:12, *RSV*). No wonder Paul is never so eloquent as when he describes the bonds of love that should exist between Christians: "[Love] is never rude or selfish; it does not take offense. . . . it is always ready to excuse, to trust, to hope, to endure whatever comes" (1 Cor. 13:5, 7). For Paul knew how division had obstructed the plan of God throughout history; Paul knew that the most destructive wound that evil could inflict on the Christian community would be to divide it.

Paul saw the weeds of division spring up almost as rapidly as the harvest of the gospel. The community at Corinth was still a newly established church when Paul had to take it to task for the divisive slogans, "I am for Paul," "I am for Apollos," "I am for Cephas" (1 Cor. 1:12). The Spirit's presence in gifts of power was no guarantee that sins of division would not destroy Christ's work.

The temptations of Corinth are no less with us today. It is easy to fall prey to mistrust; it is easy to become divided from those who take a different approach than the one we believe is right.

Paul provides a wealth of practical instruction in his letters for safeguarding the unity of the body of Christ. We must not underestimate how evil division is; we must do all within our power to prevent it from impeding the plan of God today. We must root all seeds of division out of our hearts and work anew at becoming reconciled with those from whom we are divided. We must pray for unity, as a fruit of the Spirit in our midst.

28

Lazarus

*Still sighing, Jesus reached the tomb:
it was a cave with a stone to close the
opening. Jesus said, "Take the stone
away." Martha said to him, "Lord, by
now he will smell; this is the fourth
day." Jesus replied, "Have I not told
you that if you believe you will see the
glory of God?"*

(John 11:38-40, *JB*)

Lazarus was a friend of Jesus. He was not
numbered among the apostles, but he and
his sisters, Mary and Martha, often invited Jesus
into their home in Bethany for dinner. Once
Mary sat listening to Jesus, leaving all the supper
work to Martha (Luke 10:38-42); on another occasion Mary anointed the feet of Jesus with costly
ointment (John 12:1-11). Jesus called Lazarus his
friend (John 11:11), and probably visited him
whenever his travels took him to Bethany.

Then Lazarus became sick. He and his sisters
knew of the healing power of Jesus; they knew
that Jesus could restore him to health. So they
sent word to Jesus of Lazarus's illness. They did

not beg Jesus to come and heal him: they simply sent the message, "Lord, the man you love is ill" (John 11:3). Their intimacy with Jesus and confidence in his love for them was so secure that they could simply make their needs known to Jesus, and leave everything in his hands.

But Jesus did not come. Lazarus's illness became worse, and still Jesus did not come. Finally Lazarus was at the point of death—but never a word from Jesus. What was Lazarus to think? Had Jesus abandoned him?

And then Lazarus died. His sisters went through the sad duties of burial, still awaiting word from Jesus. But as the days passed, their hopes began to dim.

Sometimes Jesus seems to delay in coming into our lives in power. We know that we are his friends. We know that we have invited him into our lives and sat down at table with him. But when we fall prey to sickness of body or spirit, Jesus can seem as far off as he seemed to be from Lazarus and Mary and Martha. We know that he is aware of our plight. Why does he not come?

If we suffer from something more serious than physical illness, we can feel ourselves like Lazarus in the tomb. We are in darkness, cut off from others by thick walls. The stone blocking our way seems too heavy to move, and we feel bound hand and foot and gagged, hardly able to even cry out for help. Our worst suffering may come from the stench of our hidden sins, a stench that we want to keep hidden from others. The walls of the tomb become our protection.

Despite the death and corruption of Lazarus, Jesus loved him: three times John's gospel assures us of this. And to remove all doubt, John gives a vivid description of the compassion of Jesus for his friend: "Jesus said in great distress, with a sigh that came straight from the heart, 'Where have you put him?'... Jesus wept.... Still sighing, Jesus reached the tomb" (11:33-34, 35, 38).

The death of Lazarus fit into the plan of God in a way that Lazarus and Mary and Martha could not understand. The death of Lazarus was not a sign that Jesus had abandoned him. Not even the stench of decay made the slightest difference to Jesus, despite Martha's polite warning. "Take the stone away... Lazarus, here! come out!... Unbind him, let him go free" (John 11:39, 43, 44). Jesus broke through the barrier of death and opened the tomb; Jesus commanded him forth and set him free of his bonds.

No matter what deadness of spirit we feel, Jesus loves us. No matter how thick the walls that enclose us and how dark the gloom that surrounds us, Jesus loves us. No matter how long we have lain helpless, and no matter how embarrassing the stench of our condition, Jesus loves us. No matter how incomprehensible the plan of God may appear to us at times, Jesus promises us life: "I am the resurrection. If anyone believes in me, even though he dies he will live, and whoever lives and believes in me will never die. Do you believe this?" (John 11:25-26).

29

Simple Things

Elisha sent him a messenger to say,
"Go and bathe seven times in the Jor-
dan, and your flesh will become clean
once more." But Naaman was indig-
nant and went off.... His servants ap-
proached him and said, "My father,
if the prophet had asked you to do
something difficult, would you not
have done it? All the more reason,
then, when he says to you, 'Bathe, and
you will become clean.'" So he went
down and immersed himself seven
times in the Jordan, as Elisha had told
him to do. And his flesh became clean
once more like the flesh of a little
child.

(2 Kings 5:10-11, 13-14, *JB*)

Naaman was a Syrian, an army commander afflicted with leprosy. He made a pilgrimage to Israel to seek healing. But Elisha did not prescribe any difficult or expensive cure for him. Elisha told him simply to bathe seven times in the Jordan River. Naaman was offended; were not the rivers of Syria as good as the rivers of Israel? He had expected to receive better treatment from the prophet than to be told to bathe in an ordinary river.

Naaman's servants persuaded him to obey anyway. After going to all the trouble of making a pilgrimage to Israel, it made sense to do something as simple as bathe in the Jordan, even if this seemed like an insulting anticlimax to his expectations. And when Naaman obeyed the prophet's simple command, he was healed of his leprosy.

Most of the things that Christ commands us to do are very simple. Some of them are even boring. But our obedience to the simple commands of Christ will make as much difference in our lives as Naaman's obedience made in his.

Jesus instructed his followers to forgive each other without limit. It is a simple thing to forgive someone who has wronged us, but a simple thing that can be very difficult to do.

"Peace be with you" was Jesus' greeting to his followers. They were to be peaceful because they were sons and daughters of his Father in heaven and therefore did not need to be worried or anxious about their lives. But we have trouble maintaining this simple perspective and so fall into worry and doubt and depression.

It is a simple thing to get up a half hour earlier in the morning and devote ourselves to prayer, or to set aside regular time each day for communion with God. Yet the impact of this simple commitment is profound. Our daily faithfulness in prayer bears fruit out of all proportion to the effort we put into it.

We may daydream about doing heroic things for God—but his requests of us may be very undramatic. We may not be called to move half way around the world to serve him; we may instead be called to love and serve people right where we are: our family, our neighbors, our co-workers. We may not be called to prominent ministries in our church or prayer group; but we may be gifted to do simple things that are important nonetheless.

When a prophet speaks in our midst today, we may be eager to hear a message revealing hidden things, promising great changes, commanding heroic action. But we know from experience that such prophecies are rare, however important they may be. Rather, the more common kind of prophetic direction we receive is an exhortation to love one another in season and out of season, a command to lay down our own desires on the altar of service to others, a promise that God is with us even in the most ordinary events of our daily lives.

Faithfulness to the simple commands of Jesus is as important as faithfulness in great things. Faithfulness to the ordinary prophetic exhortations we receive today is as important as Naaman's faithfulness to Elisha's simple instructions. Faithfulness in the simple things of each day bears dramatic fruit in a transformed life, as miraculous as Naaman rising clean from the muddy waters of the Jordan.

30

Professional Christians

It is not those who say to me, "Lord, Lord," who will enter the kingdom of heaven, but the person who does the will of my Father in heaven. When the day comes many will say to me, "Lord, Lord, did we not prophesy in your name, cast out demons in your name, work many miracles in your name?" Then I shall tell them to their faces: I have never known you; away from me, you evil men!

(Matthew 7:21-23, *JB*)

Jesus was never harsh for the sake of harshness. If his words were blunt, it was to impress an important message upon his listeners. If he called the chosen leader of the apostles "Satan," it was to jar Peter into realizing that there could be no compromise with the call of the cross. And if he called prophets, healers, and miracle workers evil men, it was to warn them that service on his behalf could never substitute for obedience to his word.

Obviously there is no contradiction between our allegiance to Christ and our service of him.

We first experience Jesus Christ as the one who brings us salvation, as the one who enables us to pray to God as our Father, as the one who pours out his Holy Spirit upon us. We accept the love of God for us; we joyfully commit our lives to Christ and set about living in obedience to the Father's will. And we set out to serve Christ, through our own efforts and through the gifts of the Spirit that we have received.

All this is as it should be. But after a period of time a subtle shift can take place. We can grow proficient in serving Christ, but lukewarm in our love of him. We can find ourselves caught up in a rapid pace of charismatic activity, but in less and less touch with God's will for us. We can be doing mighty works of healing and leading and prophesying—but no longer experience God's peace in our lives and no longer be docile to his guidance. Like the Galatians, what began in the Spirit can end in outward observances (see Gal. 3:3).

There is a danger of becoming professional Christians, focusing on works instead of relationships, on status instead of obedience, on an aspect of the Christian call instead of its essentials.

The words of Jesus call us to put first things first. The most important call we receive from God is the same call that is addressed to every man: to acknowledge that God is God, and we are his creatures; to receive the love he has for us through Jesus Christ; to be filled with the Spirit of sonship. Then it is a matter of following his will and priorities for our lives: carrying out our responsibilities of love to our families, living as brothers and sisters with other Christians, bringing the love of Jesus to the world.

A warning sign we must be alert to is a tendency to carry out charismatic activity at the expense of more basic things: when our participation in prayer meetings begins to have an adverse effect on our family life; when our pace of service leaves no time for prayer; when we feel swept along in our public role of prophet and leader, despite the voice of God growing dimmer in our personal life. Then the stern warning of Jesus must echo in our ears: it is not those who merely know how to use the right religious vocabulary who have his approval; it is not necessarily those who manifest the more extraordinary charismatic gifts, but it is those who receive the word of God into their hearts and respond to it with simple obedience whom Jesus will personally acknowledge on the day of judgment.

31

The Fruit of the Spirit

What the Spirit brings is very different: love, joy, peace, patience, kindness, goodness, trustfulness, gentleness and self-control.

(Galatians 5:22, *JB*)

Paul's list of the fruit of the Spirit is a good description of how we want to be. Instead of being worried and anxious, we would like to have a constant sense of peace. Instead of being sad or depressed, we would like to be filled with overflowing joy. Instead of being short-tempered and irritable, we wish we were patient and gentle. We would like to have complete self-control, so that we would not do things we did not want to do.

We therefore view the fruit of the Spirit as qualities that we hope to possess, qualities we will have when the sin in our lives has been eliminated and we are completely filled with the Holy Spirit.

There is another way of viewing these works of the Spirit, however. They can be understood as earmarks of our relationships with others, when we are in a loving relationship with them. The fruit of the Spirit can be understood as flourishing *between* us, as brothers and sisters in the Lord, as well as *within* us, as individual Christians.

Paul provides his own commentary on the love that the Spirit brings in 1 Corinthians 13: "Love is always patient and kind; it is never jealous; love is never boastful or conceited; it is never rude or selfish; it does not take offense, and is not resentful. Love takes no pleasure in other people's sins but delights in the truth; it is always ready to excuse, to trust, to hope, and to endure whatever comes" (4-7).

Many of these marks of love are descriptions of how we should relate to others. When we love others in the power of the Spirit, we are always ready to see the other person's point of view and to trust them; we are willing to put their good above our own; we are ready to excuse and forgive mistakes they make, without resentment. When we love others in the power of the Spirit, we will not be envious of their good fortune, even if we by contrast are in difficult times. When we are moved by love, we neither resent the success of our friends, nor gloat over their failures.

On the other hand, when we are motivated by that which is worst in us, the result is the bad fruit of "feuds and wrangling, jealousy, bad temper and quarrels; disagreements, factions, envy" (Gal. 5:20-21). Paul lists these sins along with the

manifest works of the flesh—fornication, idol-
atry, drunkenness, orgies—in contrast with the
fruit of the Spirit. And it is significant that these
bad fruits are all sins against the unity that should
exist between brothers and sisters in Christ.
Feuds and wrangling, disagreements and factions all splinter the body of Christ. Jealousy and
bad temper, quarrels and envy all break the bond
we have with each other in the Spirit.

Thus, just as the fruit of the Spirit character-
izes our unity with each other, the fruit of self-
indulgence is behavior that shatters this unity.

If we view the fruit of the Spirit as bonds between us instead of merely qualities we have in-
side ourselves, then we will try to grow in the
fruit of the Spirit in a slightly different way. Our
focus will no longer be narrowly upon ourselves,
but upon others and our relationships with them.
Our concern will be less with a spiritual self-help
program for ourselves than with the good of
others and our service of them. We will look less
at ourselves and our own spiritual condition, and
more at others, striving to love them with the sac-
rificial love of Christ. And we will find that the
more our focus is upon self-sacrificial service of
others, the better our own spiritual condition will
be. The fruit of the Spirit grows in the soil of love.

32

The Parable of the Sower

He said, "Imagine a sower going out to sow. As he sowed, some seeds fell on the edge of the path, and the birds came and ate them up. Others fell on patches of rock where they found little soil and sprang up straight away, because there was no depth of earth; but as soon as the sun came up they were scorched and, not having any roots, they withered away. Others fell among thorns, and the thorns grew up and choked them. Others fell on rich soil and produced their crop, some a hundredfold, some sixty, some thirty."

(Matthew 13:4-8, JB)

The parable of the sower conveys an important truth about the Christian life: Jesus does not merely invite us to find life in him, but also to bear fruit. The parable of the sower is a parable about fruitfulness.

There are some on whom the gospel message has little impact. Like seed dropped on a sidewalk and eaten by birds, the word of salvation never springs to life in them. And there are some who receive the gospel with eagerness and re-orient their whole lives to following and serving Jesus. Their lives bear a rich harvest for the king-dom—thirty, sixty, a hundredfold.

In between these two extremes are two other groups of people. Both eagerly receive the word at first, but bear no fruit. Both accept Jesus, but their lives do not produce the harvest that Jesus wants.

"As for what was sown on rocky ground, this is he who hears the word and immediately receives it with joy; yet he has no root in himself, but endures for a while, and when tribulation or per-secution arises on account of the word, immedi-ately he falls away" (Matt. 13:20-21, *RSV*). Jesus does not say "*if* difficulties arise" but "*when* difficulties come." And Jesus teaches that the initial joy of becoming a Christian will not be enough to sustain a person through this testing. A deeper foundation is necessary, a foundation of commitment.

"The one who received the seed in thorns is the man who hears the word, but the worries of this world and the lure of riches choke the word and so he produces nothing" (Matt. 13:22). The word is initially taken to heart, but then the con-cerns of the world sidetrack the person, and he ends up bearing no fruit.

What are the concerns of the world? For some, it may be an overriding dedication to success that leaves no room in their lives for their family, for prayer, for service. For others, it may be merely a preoccupation with trivia: spending excessive time on things not evil in themselves, but that are a distraction to fruitfulness, whether it be sports or TV or building model trains. It is hard to have a life cluttered with distractions and still be a fruitful Christian.

The parable of the sower has particular application for our times. Many today are finding new life in the Spirit and receiving the word of God into their hearts with joy. But the test comes when their initial enthusiasm has subsided, and when they are confronted with trials and difficulties. A superficial joy at knowing Jesus will most often not be enough to sustain them through the hard times. Only a profound commitment of their lives to Jesus and his service will be enough. Joy is a fruit, not a foundation.

Many do make such a commitment to Jesus Christ and enter into his service with real dedication. But then difficult choices arise—decisions about priorities, decisions about which activities must be dropped in order to have the time to serve Christ. With the pace of modern life, and with the avalanche of distractions that our society provides (many of them perfectly harmless in themselves), we must choose where to devote our time, or our fruitfulness will be choked out by the cares and lures of the world. Fruitfulness requires that our activities be reexamined, our priorities reordered, our lives reshaped, so that we have the time and energy to serve God as he has called us to serve him.

Jesus invites us to receive his word in our hearts, to commit ourselves to obeying it, to put our lives in order for his service, and to bear fruit—thirty, sixty, a hundredfold.

33

Stay with Us

When they drew near to the village to which they were going, he made as if to go on; but they pressed him to stay with them. "It is nearly evening," they said, "and the day is almost over." So he went in to stay with them. Now while he was with them at table, he took the bread and said the blessing; then he broke it and handed it to them. And their eyes were opened and they recognized him; but he had vanished from their sight.

(Luke 24:28-31, *JB*)

The scene is a familiar one. After the crucifixion of Jesus, two of his disciples are walking the road to Emmaus. They are downcast and dejected. Their hopes for the liberation of Israel have been shattered by Jesus' death. True, some of their friends visited the tomb and found it empty, and some women claimed to have seen angels who declared that Jesus was alive. But these two disciples do not know what to make of these baffling events.

Then Jesus comes and walks by their side, without their recognizing him. Jesus explains to

them how he is the fulfillment of the promises of
the prophets; he explains to them the meaning of
their scriptures, the books we read as the Old
Testament. And as he teaches them, their hearts
are touched by God's presence and love.

When they arrive at their destination they invite Jesus to stay with them. Jesus accepts their
invitation and shares a meal with them. Sudden-
ly they recognize him "in the breaking of the
bread" (24:35), and return to Jerusalem to report
what happened.

It is easy to see ourselves in these two disciples. We often have a hard time understanding
the books and prophecies of the Old Testament,
and need someone to explain them to us, just
as the disciples needed Jesus' explanation. We
sometimes have a very definite, and erroneous,
idea of what God's plan is, and become dejected
when it does not come to pass. When difficult
times come, we become downcast and depressed.
Even the encouragement and witness of friends
can fail to cut through our confusion.

But most of all, we can fail to recognize Jesus
walking by our side. Jesus can be as near to us as
he was to the two disciples on the road to Emmaus, and we can be unaware of his presence.
Perhaps at one point in our lives we seemed
close to him, just as the two disciples might have
sat at his feet when he taught in their synagogue.
But now Jesus seems absent from our lives, and
we are unsure in our faith.

The two disciples recognized Jesus in the
"breaking of the bread." When Luke uses this

term in his gospel and in Acts, he is alluding to the eucharist and teaching about that manner of Jesus' presence to his people. But it is also important to note that Jesus sat down at table with the two disciples because they invited him to: "He made as if to go on, but they pressed him to stay with them." They invited Jesus to be with them and to share a meal with them, and they consequently came to recognize his presence.

In the letter to the church at Laodicea in the book of Revelation, Christ says, "Look, I am standing at the door, knocking. If one of you hears me calling and opens the door, I will come in to share his meal, side by side with him" (Rev. 3:20). This verse is often used by evangelists to present the need for initially accepting Jesus as Lord and inviting him into our lives as our savior.

But these words were originally addressed to Christians, to those who already believe in Jesus Christ. They are an invitation for Christians to receive Jesus into their lives in a more intimate way. They are a promise that those who ask Jesus to be with them will experience his presence, just as he was present to the disciples on the road to Emmaus, and sat down with them at table.

The lesson for us is clear. Jesus already walks by our side, but we may not recognize him. He has conquered death, but our faith may be too weak to perceive it. The Father's plan of salvation has been revealed to us, but we need the inspiration of the Spirit to grasp it. Jesus awaits our invitation to enter more intimately into our lives and to open our eyes to his presence.

34

Pruning

*I am the true vine, and my Father is
the vinedresser. Every branch of mine
that bears no fruit, he takes away, and
every branch that does bear fruit he
prunes, that it may bear more fruit.*
(John 15:1-2, RSV)

Jesus in his teaching used examples that were
very familiar to his audience. When he wanted
to make a point about the kingdom of God, he
would illustrate it by talking about the size of
seeds or the problem a farmer faced in keeping
his garden free of weeds, knowing that seeds and
weeds were everyday realities to his followers.
And when Jesus wished to teach about an aspect
of his Father's love for us, he made his message
clear and vivid by talking about raising grapes.
Many of his disciples probably had grape vines
growing behind their houses and had learned
from their fathers how to care for them. Therefore
Jesus' simple words had depths of meaning for
them, depths that we who live in a more technological society often miss.

When trials or setbacks come to us in our Christian lives, we wonder why. When we are disap-

pointed or discouraged, we wonder if God still loves us, or whether he has forgotten about us. Jesus knew his followers would face such times. He told them that they would be brought to maturity and fruitfulness in the Christian life through such trials and difficulties, just as a grape vine is made more fruitful through pruning.

A good farmer does not prune *some* of his grape vines every year; he prunes all of them. He does not prune just those that have grown particularly wild; he knows that he needs to prune every vine, no matter how healthy it is, in order for it to bear the best fruit it can. And he does not prune his vines in some years but not others; grapes must be pruned every year. Pruning is a normal part of the life of a healthy grape vine.

One of the purposes of pruning is to control the amount of grapes that a vine will bear: through pruning, a vine will grow fewer but higher quality grapes. If a vine is allowed to grow without pruning, it will bud forth many more clusters of grapes than it has the strength to bring to maturity. Pruning cuts back a vine to the largest crop of grapes that it can grow well.

Our Father's pruning action in our lives has a similar function. His pruning is not a sign that he has rejected us or is gravely dissatisfied with us: it is a sign that he wants us to be healthy and bear good fruit. His pruning action is a normal part of the Christian life, not a mark that we are particularly bad or unfruitful. His pruning is not only for beginning Christians, but a continuing necessity for all of us. Sometimes his pruning forces us back to what is most important and essential in our lives, and makes us focus once again on bearing good fruit in these high priority areas.

Sometimes we are tempted to believe that we are not merely being pruned, but have become dead wood that is being cut off from the vine. Sometimes we can't see that our lives are bearing much fruit. But there are times and seasons in the Christian life, just as there are times and seasons in the life of a grape vine. Pruning takes place during the time of the year when a vine is dormant and not bearing fruit; pruning is the preparation for next year's crop. At the same time, a good vinedresser will remove any dead wood— but a good vinedresser can easily tell the difference between a branch that is dead and a branch that is merely dormant. The good vinedresser can see the signs of life beneath the apparently dead exterior, and will prune that branch so that it will bear good fruit next season.

A dead branch has no feeling, and does not know that it is being cut from the vine. Perhaps that gives us a way of knowing that we are not dead branches being cut off, but living branches being pruned: if it still hurts, we are only being pruned. And that means that the Father sees life in us, and is lovingly preparing us for our next season of harvest.

35

Friends

Jesus loved Martha and her sister and Lazarus.

(John 11:5, *JB*)

Martha and Mary and their brother, Lazarus, lived in Bethany, a small town about two miles from Jerusalem. The gospels tell us that they were friends of Jesus; there is no indication, however, that he called any of them to follow after him as traveling disciples. Rather, the gospels picture their house as a place where Jesus would stop during his travels, a place where he could get a meal, probably a place where he could rest.

Martha is portrayed as the one busy cooking and serving (Luke 10:40, John 12:2); Mary as the one who sits at Jesus' feet (Luke 10:39; John 12:3). Jesus calls Lazarus his "friend" (John 11:11), but the gospels record no words of Lazarus, and only tell us that Lazarus ate with Jesus (John 12:2) and came forth from the tomb at Jesus' command (John 11:43-44).

What did it mean to be a friend of Jesus? It must have first of all meant being his friend in

the same way that any human being is the friend
of any other human being. There was more to
the relationship between Jesus and the Bethany
household than friendship, for Martha and Mary
and Lazarus recognized Jesus as the Christ, the
Son of God (John 11:27), and recognized in him a
power over sickness and death. But the relationship between Martha and Mary and Lazarus and
Jesus was not simply one of them acknowledging him as Messiah, or revering him as a great
teacher. They were first of all friends. They liked
one another. They enjoyed being with each
other. They shared meals together, as an expression of their friendship. "Jesus loved Martha and
her sister and Lazarus."

To get an insight into this loving friendship, we
can reflect on our own experiences of friendship
and love. Who are our best friends? What kind of
affection do we feel toward them? What kinds of
things do we enjoy doing with them? When we
are reunited with a close friend after a long
separation, what emotions of joy and gladness go
through us? What sense of peace and content-
ment do we experience in simply being with a
spouse or close friend? In times of great happiness, we wish our most intimate friends could be
with us to share the joy. And in times of sorrow,
we treasure the support that comes from our
closest friends, from those we know we can depend on no matter what.

Such was the relationship between Martha
and Mary and Lazarus, and Jesus. They acknowledged him as Lord, but they also counted him as

their friend. They welcomed him to their table. They were unabashed in exhibiting their sorrow in front of him (John 11:33); their friendship was even intimate enough to involve him in their family quarrels (Luke 10:40).

Our friendship with Jesus should have the same human qualities. Just because we worship him as the Son of God does not mean that we should not strive for the same intimacy and friendship that we would with any friend. The same joy and affection that we experience in human friendship should be a part of our friendship with Jesus. The same intimacy and sharing we have with our husband or wife should characterize our relationship with Jesus. This doesn't mean we should reduce Jesus to the level of a "good buddy;" it means that he welcomes our heartfelt love as well as our worship.

We should also recognize that Jesus has the same love for us that he had toward Martha and Mary and Lazarus. If we know that our best friend has love for us and enjoys being with us, we should know that Jesus loves us even more. Jesus wants to be present at our table. He wants to share our joy, and ease our sorrow. He wants us to invite him into our lives, just as he welcomed the invitations of Martha and Mary. And he wants to be present in our lives as our Lord and redeemer—but also as our friend. "I shall not call you servants any more ... I call you friends" (John 15:15).

36

Talents

A man on his way abroad summoned his servants and entrusted his property to them. To one he gave five talents, to another two, to a third one; each in proportion to his ability. Then he set out. The man who had received the five talents promptly went and traded with them and made five more. The man who had received two made two more in the same way. But the man who had received one went off and dug a hole in the ground and hid his master's money.

(Matthew 25:14-18, *JB*)

We are familiar with how this parable turns out. The servants who made use of their master's talents were praised and rewarded by him. The servant who buried his talent was condemned, for he could at least have put the money in the bank and gained interest. And we know in a general way how this parable applies to us: we are to make use of the "talents" that God has given us for the sake of his kingdom.

There seems to be another side to the story, however. The poor servant who received only one talent was not a man of great abilities: that is why his master entrusted the smallest sum to him. We may imagine this servant deliberating about what to do with his talent: "I could try trading with it in the hope of making a profit. But then again, I might lose it if things didn't turn out right. My master would be furious with me. I could put it in the bank. But what would happen if it were embezzled, or the bank failed? There is so much about business and economics I don't understand. No, I had better play it safe and bury it. That way I won't gain anything, but I won't lose anything either."

The master condemned this servant as "wicked and lazy" and dismissed him from his service. We may find the master's action harsh. After all, the servant didn't steal the money for himself; he was simply afraid to do anything with it. He knew that he was a man of limited abilities and played it very safe.

Jesus, however, approves the master's action. After all, if the master had wanted his money buried, he could have done it himself and not bothered entrusting it to his servants. The very fact that he put his money in the care of his servants meant that he was willing for them to take risks with it. The master knew that one of his servants was a man of limited abilities, but wanted him to make the best use of those abilities that he could. The master probably would have forgiven the servant for entering into a business deal that went sour, but he had little patience with the servant being so fearful that he refused to take even the risk involved in putting the money in the bank.

It is also noteworthy that the master did not give his servants explicit instructions about what to do with the talents he gave them. He did not say to one, "Go into the shipping business," and to another, "Open up a clothing store." He left it up to them how they would invest their talents, but expected them to make the best use of them that they could.

God treats us much the same. He equips us for service to his kingdom, but usually does not dictate to us precisely how we will serve his kingdom. We must seek his will for the individual decisions we make, but usually we can use our talents to serve his kingdom in a number of different ways. Unless he gives us some special guidance, he expects us to choose the way that seems best to us, and then to work hard as his servants.

God also expects us to take risks. There is no absolutely safe way to make it through life. Committing ourselves to another person or group of people requires a risk; undertaking any kind of substantial service to the kingdom of God involves some degree of risk. We can respond to these risks fearfully, and draw back from any commitment or giving of ourselves. Or we can respond in faith, trusting that the Lord will oversee our service to him and will exercise a providential care for our lives.

The parable of the talents not only teaches us that it is important to use our gifts and abilities to serve God. It also teaches us that we must use them in faith. God may not dictate the precise way to use our talents, but he does expect us to use them on his behalf. He will forgive our mistakes but will be less patient with us if we are so fearful and untrusting that we hold back from his service. The parable of the talents teaches us about faith in action.

37

Sin

If we say we have no sin in us, we are deceiving ourselves and refusing to admit the truth; but if we acknowledge our sins, then God who is faithful and just will forgive our sins and purify us from everything that is wrong.... I am writing this, my children, to stop you sinning; but if anyone should sin, we have our advocate with the Father, Jesus Christ, who is just; he is the sacrifice that takes our sins away, and not only ours, but the whole world's.

(1 John 1:8-9, 2:1-2, *JB*)

It is uncomfortable to admit that we sin. It is much easier to admit that we make mistakes, or are weak, or do not live up to our expectations of ourselves. It is easy to carry around feelings of guilt. We try to avoid confronting ourselves with the fact that we willfully and deliberately sin, that we do things that are wrong in the eyes of God. We find it very hard to admit that some of the things we want to do and actually do are against God's commands to us, and therefore are sins.

One of the insidious results of sin is that it blinds us to itself: to the extent we sin, we are less capable of realizing that we sin. We become like a nearsighted man who has lost his glasses: if only he were wearing them, he would easily be able to see where he left them. But because he has lost them, he can't see to find them. When we are in a state of sin, we need outside help to clearly see our sin. We need God's word as a standard by which to judge ourselves: his word in scripture, his word living in his church.

"If we say we have no sin in us, we are deceiving ourselves and refusing to admit the truth." That was the tragic state of the Pharisees, and the reason they earned the most bitter denunciations of Christ. Were the Pharisees any worse sinners than anyone else Jesus dealt with? Probably not. But they stood aloof from Jesus and refused to admit their sin.

Peter, the woman taken in adultery, and many others, by contrast, all knelt at the feet of Jesus in honest acknowledgment of their sinfulness. These Jesus could forgive and heal; those who blindly refused to admit that they needed forgiveness and healing also refused to accept the forgiveness and healing that Jesus wished to bring them.

When we first turn our lives over to Jesus Christ it is easy to acknowledge the sin we want to leave behind. But it is sometimes more difficult for us to admit our sinfulness in later years, when we have been consciously trying to live the Christian life for some time. This was the problem of the Pharisees: they were religious persons by profession, so to speak. They had a self-image as holy people to maintain. It was hard for them to admit that they belonged at Jesus' feet, alongside the woman they had caught in adultery.

Jesus Christ is the sacrifice that takes away our sins. Sin is a serious enough matter in God's eyes for him to send his Son to die that sins might be forgiven. Sin is not a minor affliction that we can live with and ignore. Sin is a cancer that will end in our death if it is left untreated. The measure of the seriousness of sin is the length to which God went to redeem us from sin: the cross of Christ.

If we accept God's word of judgment and admit our sin, forgiveness is available to us through Jesus Christ. And not only forgiveness, but new life, eternal life, union with God. We need have no fear in coming before God as sinners: he knows our state, and yet welcomes us anyway. In God's eyes, the only incurable illness is the illness of refusing to admit that we are sick and need healing.

38

Creator and Father

In the beginning God created the heavens and the earth.

(Genesis 1:1, *JB*)

A book appeared some years ago with the title *Your God Is Too Small*. The God of the Hebrews was certainly not too small: he was the one who created the universe. He alone was the Lord of heaven and earth, the one who was from the beginning. The Hebrews never put Yahweh their God on an equal footing with the gods of their neighbors. Yahweh was always a transcendent God, whose name was too holy to be mentioned, whose image was too sacred to be portrayed in stone or metal.

If there was a danger in the Hebrews' awe of God it lay in removing him too far from earthly life and reducing his rule to a series of laws. The Father of Jesus, however, was no distant God. He was a God concerned about the everyday needs of his people.

Jesus taught that not even a sparrow could fall to the ground unnoticed by his Father. Therefore, how much more concerned God was with us. Jesus taught about God from his unique relationship with him as his Father—and the Son of God also provided the way for us to become children of God.

Yet despite the intimacy Jesus enjoyed with his Father, he never failed to pay him the respect due him as almighty God, creator of the universe. Jesus prayed, "I bless you, Father, Lord of heaven and of earth" (Matt. 11:25).

Paul also proclaimed God as the creator: "The God who made the world and everything in it is himself Lord of heaven and earth. . . . It is in him that we live, and move, and have our being" (Acts 17:24, 28, *JB, RSV*). The one who created us also sustains us. The one who called us forth from nothing is also the one who gives us continued life. This is a truth that we can take for granted and neglect to meditate upon. This is a truth that we can forget, and fail to draw strength from.

When we see photos of the planet Venus sent back through millions of miles of space, we may marvel at the achievements of modern science and the new vista of this world that is opened to us. But our awe should be so much more for the creator of this world than for the creation itself, for the one who endowed this world with laws that scientists could discover and exploit. We should marvel as we gaze at a starry night and realize that we can touch but one tiny portion of the universe that God created. How majestic must the Lord of heaven be, to produce such a vast creation!

The creator is also our Father. It is not as if the God we worship created the world once upon a time and then forgot about it. He so loved his creation that he sent his Son to bring it back into harmony with him. It is not as if the God we worship is a powerless God, unable to hear and answer our prayer. If God can call us forth into existence and sustain us, can he not do all else that we need? If we believe that "the world was created by one word from God" (Heb. 11:3) should we not be confident that all things are possible to our God?

The God we serve is great indeed. He is near to us as our Father, loving us with an intimate and perfect love. He is Lord of heaven and earth, almighty God, creator of all that exists. He sustains us in life; his love is constant and dependable; he is by our side for us to call upon him. The creator is our Father.

39

Gifts Freely Given

So I say to you: Ask, and it will be given to you; search, and you will find; knock, and the door will be opened to you. For the one who asks always receives; the one who searches always finds; the one who knocks will always have the door opened to him. What father among you would hand his son a stone when he asked for bread? Or hand him a snake instead of a fish? Or hand him a scorpion if he asked for an egg? If you then, who are evil, know how to give your children what is good, how much more will the heavenly Father give the Holy Spirit to those who ask him!

(Luke 11:9-13, *JB*)

We usually consider spiritual gifts and personal talents as capabilities that we have been given by the Lord, independent of our deserving them. Some of us are gifted in administration; others are talented in music; others receive prophetic messages; still others have a writing ability. All these different gifts and abilities can be used to help carry out the mission of the church. But we know that we did not earn or deserve the special gift or ability we have received. Our gifts from the Lord are simply that: gifts, freely given.

Unfortunately we sometimes carry our thinking a step farther with the attitude that we should not desire or ask for spiritual gifts. But this is a mistake. While we can't earn them, we can and should ask for them.

Paul wrote to the church at Corinth: "Be ambitious for the higher gifts. . . . By all means be ambitious to prophesy" (1 Cor. 12:31; 14:39). Paul taught that the way of love was the highest way of all. But he also taught that it was proper to desire and pray for spiritual gifts, including prophecy and the gift of interpretation (see 1 Cor. 14:13).

What gifts should we desire? We should ask for the ones that would be of greatest use to our local Christian community. Our aim should be to serve, and therefore to be equipped to perform our service. We should be guided by the needs of the community, rather than our own personal ambition, in asking for gifts.

Paul taught that there is a wide variety of spiritual gifts including some that we might not normally think of as spiritual gifts: administration and helping, for example (1 Cor. 12:28). It may be that we are needed to serve in some capacity that does not require a very spiritual-looking gift. If our opportunity to serve is in visiting the sick, then we should ask to be equipped to serve with genuine love and patience and sympathy, and an ease at praying with the sick for healing. If we serve on a council or commission or leaders group, we might pray for skills of administration.

But above all, in asking for gifts we should keep in mind the needs of the community. Do we need to hear God's prophetic word addressed to us more frequently and clearly? Then we should pray that a gift of prophecy will be given—to us or to someone else in our group. Is our need for Bible teaching, for simple and practical exposition of the scriptures? Then we should pray for that gift to be given, and to receive it personally if that is how we are called to serve. Is there a need for a greater demonstration of God's power in our midst? Then we should not be reluctant to pray for the gift of healing, not because we aspire to be a healer but because that gift would strengthen the witness of God in our community. We should pray as a community for the gifts the community needs; we should pray as individuals for the gifts we need to serve.

We should pray for gifts with confidence. We can't earn gifts, but we *can* ask for them. Jesus taught us that we should ask for them with confidence, trusting that our heavenly Father hears our requests. If we know what to provide our children so that they can grow to adulthood, even more our Father in heaven knows what the church needs to carry out its mission. If our aim is to serve the church, we can be confident that our prayer will be heard as we ask for the gifts and graces and talents needed for us to serve the church.

40

The Spirit in the Church

Then some men came down from Judea and taught the brothers, "Unless you have yourselves circumcised in the tradition of Moses you cannot be saved." This led to disagreement, and after Paul and Barnabas had had a long agrument with these men it was arranged that Paul and Barnabas and others of the church should go up to Jerusalem and discuss the problem with the apostles and elders.

(Acts 15:1-2, *JB*)

The church on Pentecost day was a Jewish church, made up of the followers that Jesus had left behind in Jerusalem when he ascended into heaven. After Pentecost the gospel quickly spread beyond Judea, however, to cities like Antioch, and soon gentiles began to believe in the good news about Jesus Christ. This raised questions: did non-Jewish converts to Christianity also have to become converts to Judaism? Were they also to be bound by the law of Moses?

The explicit teachings of Jesus while he was on earth did not resolve these questions. He had conducted his public ministry mainly within the borders of Israel, and he had addressed his message primarily to the descendants of Abraham. Hence, unanswered questions faced the early church, especially as a result of the missionary efforts of St. Paul.

On the surface, this state of affairs is surprising. Surely Jesus should have realized that his instruction to "make disciples of all the nations" (Matt. 28:19) would raise the question whether these disciples were to follow the law of Moses that he himself had respected. And surely Jesus could have resolved the question with a few simple, direct words. But there is no record that he did, and the evidence of the New Testament is that he did not. We must wonder, why didn't he?

Although Jesus did not leave behind explicit instructions that would have prevented the first serious crisis in the church, he did provide the means for resolving this and all future crises the church would face. He left behind a group of men that he had given his authority to. And he sent his Holy Spirit upon them to guide them as they guided his church.

After Paul and Barnabas reached Jerusalem, a prolonged debate occurred over the gentile-convert question. "After the discussion had gone on a long time" (Acts 15:7), Peter decisively intervened, siding with Paul. Then James, who was apparently the presiding elder of the Jerusalem church, made a pronouncement which began, "I rule, then . . . " (Acts 15:19). And so a letter was drafted that conveyed the stand of Peter and James, a letter which was to be binding on the

Christian communities that had sent Paul and Barnabas to Jerusalem with their questions. The letter stated, "It has been decided by the Holy Spirit and by ourselves" that gentile converts are not bound by the prescriptions of the Mosaic law (Acts 15:28).

So the matter was resolved not by the explicit teachings of Jesus but by the men he had placed in authority over his church, under the guidance of the Holy Spirit. Jesus left behind a body of basic teaching, valid for all time, but he knew that he could not possibly address the innumerable questions that would face the church throughout the ages. So he did not attempt to resolve them himself. Instead he left behind his authority and his Spirit, operating in those responsible for guiding his church.

The plan adopted by Jesus should be a source of confidence for us. Not only have we received the teachings of Jesus from his years on earth, but we have received the presence of the Holy Spirit, working through those who have been given the mission of guiding the church. We can have confidence in the word of God to us, which we read in scripture. And we can also have confidence that this word is heard and applied today by those in authority over the church. We can have the same confidence that the Christian communities in Antioch and Syria and Cilicia had when they received the letter from Jerusalem. They were confident that the Holy Spirit had spoken through Peter and James. We can be confident that the same Holy Spirit guides the church today.

41

The Meaning of Repentance

*Jesus began his preaching with the
message, "Repent, for the kingdom of
heaven is close at hand."*
(Matthew 4:17, JB)

When we think of repentance, we usually
think of forsaking sin. If there is serious
sin in our life, we hear the call to repentance as a
call to commit that sin no longer. The call to repentance certainly involves this, but it also involves something much more fundamental.

Repentance is a translation of the Greek word
used in scripture, *metanoia*. Metanoia means a
change of heart, a change of mind. It thus means
something deeper than a change in our external
actions: it means a change within ourselves, a
change of that which is the source of our behavior. It means a change of our whole orienta-
tion, our way of thinking, our values and priorities. It means adopting a new goal for our lives, a
goal that determines how we act.

The radical nature of the call to repentance is
made clear by the later teaching of Jesus. "He

called the people and his disciples to him and said, 'If anyone wants to be a follower of mine, let him renounce himself and take up his cross and follow me. For anyone who wants to save his life will lose it; but anyone who loses his life for my sake, and for the sake of the gospel, will save it. What gain, then, is it for a man to win the whole world and ruin his life?' " (Mark 8:34-36).

Jesus demands a total reversal of our normal way of thinking and our instinctive values. We are inclined to want the best for ourselves, to place our good over that of others, to weigh every decision in terms of the benefits for ourselves. Even if our lives are not completely dominated by the urge to acquire money and possessions, there is still in us the childish temptation to want the biggest cookie on the plate of life. Even if we are not ruthless in our pursuit of getting ahead, we still have a hard time putting the success of others ahead of our own.

The repentance Jesus calls for is a reorientation of this instinctive urge to put ourselves first. Jesus calls for a conversion from relying on our own talents and resources to relying upon his care for us. The repentance Jesus calls for involves making him the Lord of our lives instead of ourselves.

If we understand Jesus' call to repentance in this way, some of the other teachings of Jesus take on added significance. The drive to accumulate wealth can be seen as an expression of self-sufficiency, a desire to make one's future secure against all dangers. But this is as much folly as trying to march a camel through the eye of a needle. True security does not lie in what we possess but in what we give up; true security lies not in faith in our own resources but in faith in Jesus Christ. The self-satisfied attitude of the Pharisees can be seen as a refusal to repent, a refusal to give up all attempts at self-righteousness for the righteousness that Jesus gives. The Pharisee trusted in his own efforts to save his life, but only those who lose their lives by handing them over to God will save them.

Repentance is a reorientation of our lives. Repentance is grasping hold of the paradoxical truth that he who would save his life must embrace the losing of it. Repentance is reversing our natural set of priorities and living according to the values that Jesus taught.

The call to repentance therefore goes much deeper than turning aside from obvious sins. The need for repentance is a lifelong need, because it is the process of continually placing our lives in the hands of God. It is the continual process of putting Jesus and his kingdom first, in our daily decisions and in the long-range direction of our lives, in our thoughts and in our desires. Repentance is the daily taking up of the cross of Jesus, so that we may follow in his footsteps.

42

Faith

*Then he spoke to Thomas, "Put your
finger here; look, here are my hands.
Give me your hand; put it into my
side. Doubt no longer but believe."
Thomas replied, "My Lord and my
God!" Jesus said to him: "You believe
because you can see me. Happy are
those who have not seen and yet believe."*

*There were many other signs that
Jesus worked and the disciples saw,
but they are not recorded in this book.
These are recorded so that you may
believe that Jesus is the Christ, the Son
of God, and that believing this you
may have life through his name."*

(John 20:27-31, *JB*)

John's gospel was the last one to be written,
probably composed during the last decades of
the first century. John wrote for those who had
not known Jesus during his life on earth but had
heard the message of salvation from the apostles
and their successors.

The incident of Thomas's doubting that Jesus was truly risen and alive, therefore, had a special meaning for those that first read John's gospel. They had not seen Jesus during the years he walked the paths of Galilee; they had not heard him teach in the temple. Yet because of the preaching of the church, they had come to believe that Jesus was truly alive and reigning as Lord. This incident in John's gospel commended them for their faith, they who had not physically seen Jesus after his resurrection yet still believed in him.

John's gospel is written equally for us. It makes no difference whether we are one generation or one hundred generations removed from the day when Jesus rose from the dead; we are basically in the same situation as those John wrote for. He wrote so that we too might believe that Jesus reigns as Lord, and so that we too might receive life from him.

The reign and presence of Jesus is not very obvious in the world today. When we read our daily paper or watch the news on TV, what counts as news is all too often tragedy and suffering. God seems to be systematically left unmentioned, as if he did not exist or as if he were a theory held by a minority of people. It is not that our culture is explicitly antireligious; rather it simply acts as if Jesus never lived and does not live now.

Our own awareness of the presence of Jesus can become gradually dimmed. Most of our waking hours are taken up by the many tasks we have to do. We know that we can go for stretches of time without even thinking of God. It is not that we want to ignore him. But he is not present to us with the insistence of children clamoring to be fed, or customers to be served, or letters to be answered. At times we are almost physically aware of the presence of Jesus—but at other times, it is as if he had vanished from our lives.

Life was probably no less distracting in the Roman empire. John certainly did not write for those living in a culture any more Christian than our own. Nor has the nature of being a follower of Jesus changed any in the last 1900 years. Jesus was not present to the Christians living toward the end of the first century in any way that he is not present to us. We can therefore take the Thomas incident as being in a special way written for us today, and carrying a particular word of encouragement for us.

Our faith is not in any way defective because we do not physically see Jesus. Faith is precisely in the unseen. St. Paul terms it the "conviction of things unseen" (Heb. 11:1) and states that "we walk by faith, not by sight" (2 Cor. 5:7).

And there is a special blessing of Jesus for those who do not see yet believe. There is a special love of Jesus for those who persevere in their faith in him, despite the unbelief around them and the distractions of their lives. They are the ones who have found life in the name of Jesus: who have welcomed the message of the gospel and confessed to Jesus, "My Lord and my God."

43

Signs and Wonders

Oh, that you would tear the heavens
open and come down
—at your Presence the mountains
would melt,
as fire sets brushwood alight,
as fire causes water to boil—
to make known your name to your
enemies,
and make the nations tremble at
your Presence,
working unexpected miracles
such as no one has ever heard of
before.

(Isaiah 64:1-3)

Chapters 63 and 64 of the book of Isaiah contain a psalm apparently written during the time of the exile. The psalm laments the condition of the chosen people, asking why the tragedy of the exile happened. Why had God allowed his people to stray from him? Why had God allowed the destruction of his temple? "Your holy cities are a wilderness ... our holy and glorious temple ... is burnt to the ground.... Yahweh, can you go unmoved by all of this, oppressing us beyond measure by your silence?" (Isa. 64:9, 10, 11).

The psalm begs God to be present in power, to clearly demonstrate his dominion by signs and wonders: "Tear the heavens open and come down," melting mountains, making the world tremble at the awesome manifestation. The psalm asks God to work unheard-of miracles, removing all doubt of his lordship over the earth.

It is easy to long for the same kind of demonstration of the power of God today. Much of the world does not acknowledge the existence of God and the lordship of Jesus Christ. Many of the followers of Jesus seem disheartened and lukewarm. If God is the creator of the universe, could he not level a few mountain ranges as a demonstration of his power? Could he not work some cosmic sign to prove his existence to the skeptical and indifferent? Could he not loose a few thunderbolts to bolster the faith of his followers?

God did end the exile of his chosen people and return them to the promised land—but he accomplished this through human instruments. He did not melt mountains to demonstrate his power; he did not destroy the walls of Babylon with a thunderbolt to free his people. Instead he made use of a Persian king, Cyrus, who captured Babylon and sent the Israelites home. He made use of men like Ezra and Nehemiah to restore the walls of Jerusalem and rebuild the temple.

We may long for God to obliterate the Himalayan mountains as a sign that would bring about the conversion of China, but that does not seem to be a part of his plan. We may long for more spectacular signs and wonders to be worked in our prayer meetings—but signs and wonders are not necessarily the most fitting demonstration of the presence of God. The main indication of the presence and power of God is in the transformed lives of his followers.

Jesus worked miracles during his public ministry, but his emphasis was on forming his disciples to be his body. Jesus did not even choose to perform the more spectacular wonders that must have been at his disposal: if his followers could pray with faith to cast a mountain into the sea, surely Jesus himself could have done this, if such a sign would have silenced the Pharisees and converted the indifferent. But Jesus chose to carry out his mission by forming a people. He chose to have his Spirit remain present in the world in the lives of men and women.

God chooses to work through human instruments, even to demonstrate his power. The sign of God's presence is the love that exists among his followers. The astonishing wonder to be seen is the unity of those who have found life in his name. In God's plan, we are to be his miracle in the world today.

44

The Perspective of Eternity

*"It is my Father's will that whoever
sees the Son and believes in him shall
have eternal life, and that I shall raise
him up on the last day."*

(John 6:40)

These words of Jesus transform the meaning of
human life. They challenge every natural as-
sumption and value we might hold. They require
us to radically change our perspective on what is
important and what is unimportant.

According to our natural view, life ends with
death. Death comes as a tragic separation between lover and beloved, between child and parent, between life-long friends. Death disrupts the
highest human happiness we can experience, the
love of two persons for each other.

Sometimes death comes out of season, taking
away a young person barely setting out on life.
Sometimes death takes away someone we were
counting on to help us: a political leader able to
arouse hope, a scientist working on a cure for
cancer, a writer able to inspire us. And sometimes death comes sadly late and out of season,

after an elderly person has declined far from being the person they once were.

If our present life is but a prelude, however, our perspective is radically changed. Then there is no permanent separation between those united in love in Christ. Then there is no such thing as a death too early or a death too late. Then we need not lose hope for those whose last years are years of decline: they shall once again be the persons they were, and more. They shall experience a resurrection of their body that frees them from the accumulated disabilities of decades; they shall once again rejoice in the fullness of life.

The perspective of eternity must also transform our view of all who live in our midst who seem to be short-changed by life. Those born mentally retarded must seem condemned to be incomplete persons, unless we can anticipate their completion in eternity. Those who are victims of incurable diseases and birth defects, consigned to a life of dependence, must seem to us cruelly robbed of life, unless we know in faith that such greater fulfillment awaits us all that their suffering will be made up 100 times over.

The perspective of eternity must also shape our view of the unborn. If no spark of human life will ever die out, then the unborn must be reverenced for their life as well as the born. If God can raise up with new bodies those whose earthly bodies are deformed and ravaged, then he can certainly also give resurrected bodies even to those whose earthly bodies never had a chance to develop fully.

The prospect of eternal life must also change our evaluation of those whose earthly life is one of poverty and suffering. We can have hope that those whose present life is one of misery will find rest and reward in the next life. But even more, our prospect of sharing eternal life with them must change our perspective of our obligation to them here and now. I cannot turn my back on the starvation of refugees on the other side of the world; I shall be with them in eternity, and must be concerned for them now.

There will be a judgment for each of us as we enter eternal life. We must live in hope of passing that judgment, through the redemption that Jesus Christ has given us. We must also hold that hope for others, that they too will be saved through the mystery of God's love for them. Then our expectation can be that those we love now, we will be able to love for all eternity. Our hope can be that those who do not experience the fullness of life on this earth will experience it in the presence of their Father in heaven. Then our obligation must be to reverence everyone as intended for resurrection into eternal life with us, in Christ Jesus our Lord.